FLYING OVER EUROPE
The Netherlands

Introduction by H.R.H. Prince Bernhard of the Netherlands

Compiled and edited by Henk Siliakus

Aerial photography:
  Aerophoto Schiphol B.V.

Caption-drafts and research:
  M. Willemsen

Translations:
  Art & Information, Bergen (N.H.)

Typesetting:
  Vrieset B.V., Alkmaar

Colour separations:
  Scan Studio, Heemstede

Printed in the Netherlands/Imprimé en Hollande:
  Boom-Ruygrok Offset B.V., Haarlem

Binding:
  Albracht Brandt Binderijen B.V., Montfoort

Published by Promo Mundi B.V., Alkmaar
ISBN 90-72317-03-3
NUGI 672/675

FLYING OVER EUROPE
The Netherlands

Publishers: Promo Mundi B.V.,
P.O. Box 8172 - 1812 KD Alkmaar

For Bob Naylor.   Febr. '95

In remembrance of the
pleasant contacts and fine
cooperation during many
years

God bless You.

Roel Wolting

Introduction by
H.R.H. Prince Bernhard
of the Netherlands

pages 6-11:

*English, Dutch,
German, French,
Spanish and Japanese*

*H.R.H. Prince Bernhard at the controls of the governmental aeroplane,
the Fokker F28 PH-PBX.*

(photo: B. Straatman, Soesterberg Airbase)

When I was asked to write an introduction in this aerial photo book, I consented at once, mainly for the following reasons:

First of all I have been flying planes for the past 48 years and observed the Netherlands from many different types of aircraft and often at low altitudes. This bird's-eye view of the Dutch landscape, beautiful towns and our industry, so splendidly reproduced in this book, the average air-traveller rarely enjoys. Therefore, in my opinion, this publication of skilfully photographed and neatly arranged objects, offers a surprising panorama.

Secondly this book shows a great deal more than predictable shots such as windmills which people of other nations traditionally associate with Holland. It also illustrates the manner in which, through centuries, we have outwitted wind and wave by means of knoll villages, sea walls and Delta Works, like our most recent national achievement: the Great Flood Barrier of the East Scheldt.

Thirdly also because of the pride one feels as a Dutchman by looking at all those things our beautiful, yet small country has to offer.

Prince of the Netherlands

Toen men mij vroeg een voorwoord in dit luchtfotoboek te willen schrijven, heb ik zonder aarzeling "ja" gezegd en wel om verschillende redenen.

Ten eerste ben ik nu al 48 jaren vlieger en heb ik vanuit vele vliegtuigtypen Nederland menigmaal laagvliegend kunnen bekijken. Deze kijk op het Nederlandse landschap, stedenschoon en industrie, die zo fraai in dit boek is weergegeven, heeft de gemiddelde luchtreiziger nauwelijks. Daarom biedt deze uitgave van vakkundig gefotografeerde en gerangschikte onderwerpen mijns inziens een verrassend panorama.

Ten tweede wordt nu eens niet alleen aandacht besteed aan de doorsnee-onderwerpen zoals molens e.d., die bij veel buitenlanders worden ervaren als iets typisch Hollands, maar wordt ook getoond hoe wij sinds eeuwen hebben moeten vechten tegen de elementen, getuige de terpendorpen, zeeweringen en de deltawerken, met onze laatste nationale aanwinst: de stormvloedkering in de Oosterschelde.

Ten derde ook vanwege de trots die men als Nederlander voelt bij het bekijken van al dat moois dat ons toch kleine land te bieden heeft.

Prins der Nederlanden

Als man mich bat, ein Vorwort zu diesem Luftbildband zu schreiben, habe ich ohne zu zögern zugestimmt, und zwar aus mehreren Gründen.

Erstens bin ich nun schon seit 48 Jahren Flieger und habe mir aus so manchem Flugzeugtyp die Niederlande viele Male aus der Vogelschau anschauen können. Dem durchschnittlichen Luftpassagier bietet sich die in diesem Band so schön dargestellte niederländische Landschaft mit ihren prächtigen Städten und ihrer Industrie in dieser Perspektive wohl kaum. Somit enthält dieser Band mit meisterhaft fotografierten und angeordneten Themen meines Erachtens ein Panorama voller Überraschungen.

Zweitens wird mit diesem Werk dem etwas stereotypen Bild der Windmühlen u.ä., das viele Ausländer als typisch für die Niederlande erfahren, keine ausschließliche Aufmerksamkeit geschenkt. Denn es wird gezeigt, wie wir uns seit vielen Jahrhunderten gegen die Naturgewalten zur Wehr haben setzen müssen. Zeugen dafür sind die Wurtendörfer, Küstenbefestigungsanlagen und die Deltawerke mit unserer letzten großen Errungenschaft - das Sturmflutwehr in der Oosterschelde.

Und drittens, weil man als Niederländer stolz ist, wenn man sich all das Schöne zu Gemüte führt, das unser kleines Land zu bieten hat.

Prinz der Niederlande

Contents

13

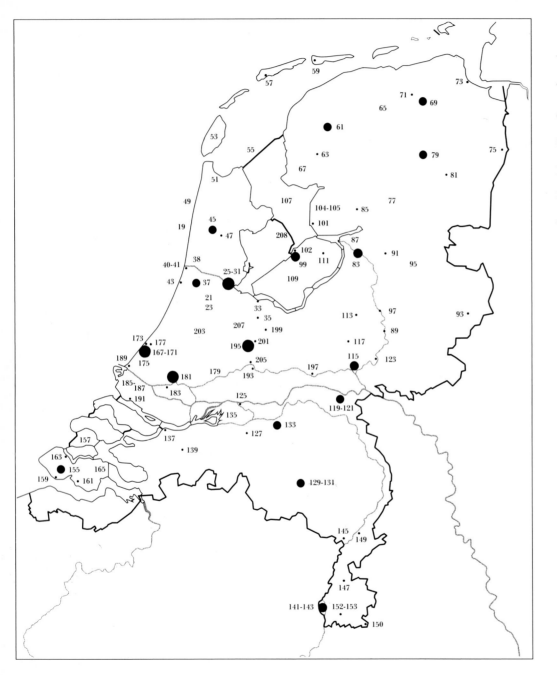

Location Indications

The numbers on the map correspond with the numbers of the photo pages as they appear in the contents, listed on pages 13-15.

The aerial photographs

In compiling this book,
a careful selection has been
made from the available and
recently photographed scenes.

Although it was impossible to
show each and every place in the
Netherlands, the contents cover
a great deal of the various
aspects our beautiful country
has to offer.

An air to air shot of the photoplane of KLM Luchtfotografie, the Cessna 172 PH-OTK.

Endless clouds over the Dutch coast near Egmond

Almost endlessly, clouds seem to be drifting in over the coast of Holland. Ever changing patterns often bringing welcome rains which keep the Low Lands so lavishly green.
Descending to Schiphol the air travellers catch a first glimpse of the Netherlands feeling satisfied to have reached their destination.

Schier eindeloos lijken wolken binnen te drijven over de Hollandse kust. Van een steeds veranderend patroon en een vaak welkome regen met zich meebrengend, die de Lage Landen zo kwistig groen houdt.
Tijdens de afdaling naar Schiphol vangen de luchtreizigers een eerste blik op van Nederland, met het voldane gevoel hun bestemming bereikt te hebben.

In scheinbar endlosen Karawanen ziehen die Wolken über die niederländische Küste. In ständig wechselnden Mustern, und oft den begehrten Regen mit sich führend, dem die Niederlande ihr üppiges Grün zu verdanken haben.
Beim Anflug auf Schiphol, dem Amsterdamer Flughafen, erhaschen die Luftpassagiere einen ersten Blick der Niederlande, froh darüber, den Bestimmungsort erreicht zu haben.

La côte hollandaise... couverte de nuages passant presque sans fin. Changeant de forme sans cesse, ils apportent la pluie souvent souhaitée, qui donne au pays sa riche verdure.
En descendant vers l'aéroport de Schiphol, les passagers aperçoivent pour la première fois une partie des Pays-Bas et éprouvent la satisfaction complète d'avoir atteint leur destination.

Casi sin cesar, las nubes parecen adentrarse flotando sobre la costa holandesa. Tienen contornos siempre cambiantes y traen consigo lluvias que a menudo son bienvenidas, por las que los Países Bajos siguen siendo tan abundantemente verdes.
En el descenso hacia Schiphol, los viajeros aéreos obtienen una primera impresión de Holanda, sintiéndose satisfechos de haber alcanzado su destino.

たゆみなくオランダの沿岸に浮き漂う雲。オランダの雲は変化に満ちた模様を織りなし、この低い国の豊かな緑を保つ恵みの雨をもたらす。
スキポール・アムステルダム国際空港への降下が始まると、目的地に着きつつある満足感とともに、飛行機の乗客はオランダの第一印象を目におさめます。

Schiphol Airport

Schiphol has been declared more than once to be the best equipped airport in the world. On a piece of marshland in the Haarlemmermeer polder it was initially a military airfield from 1917-1920.

Because of its central location in Europe and through the accommodation offered, Schiphol developed rapidly into what it is today: an airport of great capacity and world fame.

Schiphol werd reeds menigmaal verklaard de best geoutilleerde luchthaven ter wereld te zijn. Op een stuk moeras in de Haarlemmermeer polder, was het aanvankelijk een militair vliegveld van 1917-1920.

Vanwege de centrale ligging in Europa en de geboden accommodatie, groeide Schiphol al snel uit tot wat het tegenwoordig is: een luchthaven van grote omvang en wereldfaam.

Schiphol wurde bereits mehrmals zum bestaugerüsteten Flughafen der Welt erklärt. Auf einem Stück Sumpfland im Haarlemmermeer-Polder war es von 1971 bis 1920 zunächst ein Militärflughafen.

Wegen seiner Zentrallage innerhalb Europas und wegen des gebotenen Komforts entwickelte Schiphol sich rasch zu dem, was es heute ist: ein Flughafen von großem Umfang und mit Weltruhm.

Schiphol, vanté si souvent pour son équipement superbe, était un aéroport militaire de 1917 à 1920, construit sur un marais dans le Haarlemmermeerpolder.

Situé favorablement au centre de l'Europe et offrant une carlinque confortable, Schiphol s'est étendu à ses dimensions actuelles: un aéroport important jouissant d'une réputation mondiale.

Schiphol fue declarado más de una vez el aeropuerto mejor equipado del mundo. Habilitado sobre un terreno pantanoso desecado del pólder Haarlemmermeer, fue en sus orígenes, de 1917 a 1920, un aeródromo militar.

Gracias a su situación central dentro de Europa y al alojamiento que ofrece, Schiphol creció rápidamente hasta lo que es hoy en día: un aeropuerto con una gran capacidad y de fama mundial.

スキポール・アムステルダム国際空港は、幾度も世界一設備の整った空港として選出されました。ハーレミアー湖干拓地の沼地であったこの地は、最初1917年から1920年にかけて、軍用空港として使用されていました。

ヨーロッパの中心を占める立地条件と優秀な設備によって、スキポールは短期間で現在の、高い知名度と使いやすさで定評をもつ空港となりました。

Aalsmeer, The Flower Auction

The United Flower Auction Aalsmeer has every right to be called the largest of its kind in the world. First of all because of the building itself, with a complex of halls, totalling 630.000 square meters.
Further because of the number of cut-flowers and plants being auctioned daily. The figures: 12.6 million cut-flowers and over 1.3 million plants in hundreds of varieties!

De "Verenigde Bloemenveilingen Aalsmeer" (VBA) mag zich met recht de grootste bloemenveiling ter wereld noemen. Ten eerste vanwege het gebouw zelf, met een hallencomplex van circa 630.000 m². Verder vanwege het aantal snijbloemen en planten dat dagelijke wordt geveild. De cijfers: 12.6 miljoen snijbloemen en meer dan 1.3 miljoen planten in honderden variëteiten!

Die "Vereinigten Blumenversteigerungen Aalsmeer" dürfen sich mit Recht die größte Blumen-versteigerung der Welt nennen. Erstens wegen des Gebäudes und den Hallen mit einer Gesamtfläche von ca. 630.000 m².
Und zweitens wegen der Anzahl Schnittblumen und Pflanzen, die hier tagaus tagein versteigert werden. Die Zahlen: 12,6 Mio. Schnittblumen und über 1,3 Mio. Pflanzen in vielen hunderten Varietäten!

L' "Association des ventes aux enchères de fleurs" peut être nommée, à juste titre, la plus grande du monde. D'abord, grâce au grand complexe de halles de 630.000 m².
Ensuite, au grand nombre de fleurs coupées (12.6 millions) et de plantes (1.3 millions) qui y sont vendues chaque jour en centaines de variations!

Las Subastas Unidas de Flores de Aalsmeer pueden calificarse con razón como las mayores subastas de flores del mundo. Esto se debe en primer lugar al edificio mismo, con un complejo de naves de alrededor de 630.000 metros cuadrados.
Además, a causa del gran número de flores cortadas y plantas que salen a subasta todos los días. Las cifras: 12,6 millones de flores cortadas y más de 1,3 millones de plantas en centenares de variedades!

アールスメア生花中央市場共同組合は、世界一の生花市場です。まず建物そのものが63万平方メートルで、後楽園の約11倍にもおよびます。
また毎日セリで扱う生花と観葉植物の数も世界一で、生花が1260万本、数百種にわたる観葉植物が130万鉢となっています。

Amsterdam, Town- and Music Hall

In the historic heart of Amsterdam on the banks of the river Amstel the new Town and Music Hall was founded. The 'skinny bridge' can also be clearly seen in the foreground of the aerial photo.

Even before the opening of the Town Hall section in September 1988 this remarkable building, housing totally different activities, became known at home and abroad as 'The Stopera'.

In het historische hart van Amsterdam, verrees aan de Amstel - op de luchtfoto is ook heel duidelijk de "magere brug" te zien - het nieuwe Stadhuis/Muziektheater.

Zelfs vóór de opening van het Gemeentehuis in September 1988, werd dit markante gebouw, met zijn veelsoortige activiteiten heel bekend - ook in het buitenland - onder de bijnaam "De Stopera".

Im historischen Teil der Stadt Amsterdam wurde am Ufer der Amstel das neue Rathaus/Konzertgebäude erbaut; auf dem Luftbild erkennt man übrigens ganz deutlich die "Magere Brücke".

Sogar noch vor der Eröffnung des Rathaustrakts im September 1988 wurde dieses markante Gebäude mit seinen vielen diversen Aktivitäten auch im Ausland unter dem Beinamen "Stopera" bekannt.

Au centre historique d'Amsterdam, aux bords de l'Amstel, s'élève le nouvel hôtel de ville/le nouvel Opéra - la photo aérienne montre aussi nettement le "pont maigre".

Même avant son ouverture en septembre 1988, le bâtiment remarquable - surnommé "Le Stopera" - avait une réputation internationale grâce à ses activités multiples.

En el histórico corazón de Amsterdam se construyó el nuevo Ayuntamiento/Salón de Conciertos, a orillas del río Amstel - en la fotografía aérea puede también verse claramente el 'puente delgado'.

El destacado edificio, con sus múltiples actividades, se hizo muy famoso - también fuera del país - bajo el sobrenombre de 'La Stópera', aun antes de inaugurarse el Ayuntamiento en septiembre de 1988.

この航空写真の最前部は、「やせっぽちの橋」という意味のマーハラ橋です。古い歴史を誇るアムステルダムのアムステル川沿いに、新市庁舎と、ミュージックホールが建造されました。

1988年9月に民事課がオープンする以前から、この「ストペラ」というニックネームを持ち、各種の活動の地点となってるユニークな建物は、国内でも外国でも有名になりました。

Amsterdam, World Trade Center

In constructing the 'World Trade Center', also known as the 'Blue Angel', Amsterdam created a most important international business centre. Located in the south of the Dutch capital in Strawinsky Lane it accommodates about 300 trade firms.

This modern, glass building truly reflects Amsterdam's historic trading tradition.

Door het bouwen van het "World Trade Center", ook bekend als de "Blauwe Engel", heeft Amsterdam een zeer belangrijk internationaal handelscentrum gecreëerd. Gelegen in het Zuidelijk deel van de hoofdstad van Nederland, aan de Strawinskylaan, biedt het onderdak aan circa 300 handelsfirma's.

Dit moderne glazen gebouw reflecteert daadwerkelijk Amsterdams' historische handelstraditie.

Mit dem Bau des "World Trade Centers", im Volksmund der "Blaue Engel", schuf Amsterdam sich ein sehr wichtiges internationales Handelszentrum. Das im Süden der niederländischen Hauptstadt an der Strawinskylaan gelegene Gebäude beherbergt zirka 300 Handelsfirmen.

In diesem modernen Glasbau reflektiert sich Amsterdams historische Handelstradition.

Grâce à la création du "World Trade Center", dit l'"Ange Bleu", Amsterdam a connu un grand intérêt international comme centre d'affaires. Situé dans la partie du sud de la capitale, dans l'avenue Strawinsky, il abrite environ 300 entreprises commerciales.

Sa construction moderne en verre reflète la longue tradition commerciale d'Amsterdam.

Con la construcción del "World Trade Center", también conocido como el 'Angel Azul', Amsterdam ha creado un centro comercial international de gran importancia. Ubicado en la parte meridional de la capital holandesa, en la Strawinskylaan, alberga alrededor de 300 casas comerciales.

Este moderno edificio de vidrio refleja realmente la histórica tradición comercial de Amsterdam.

ワールド・トレード・センターは「青い天使」という名でも知られていますが、アムステルダムで最も重要な国際ビジネス・センターです。首都アムステルダムの南部のストラビンスキー通りに設立されたこの建物には、貿易関連企業約300社があります。

この近代的なガラス建築は、アムステルダムの長い商業の伝統のシンボルでもあります。

Amsterdam, Postal Sorting Centre near Central Station

The Postal Sorting Centre in Amsterdam is attractively situated at the IJ harbour and conveniently close to Central Station for the national and international forwarding of mail. Also via Schiphol Airport by means of a direct rail link (the Schiphol Line).
   Each working day the 'PTT Post' copes with millions of letters and parcels, largely automatically.

Het expeditieknooppunt van de PTT in Amsterdam is fraai gelegen aan het IJ en heel effectief dichtbij het Centraal Station, ten behoeve van de nationale en buitenlandse postexpeditie, ook via Schiphol, door middel van een directe spoorlijnverbinding (de Schiphollijn).
   Elke werkdag verwerkt "PTT Post" - grotendeels geautomatiseerd - miljoenen poststukken.

Die Verteilungsstelle der niederländischen "PTT Post" in Amsterdam liegt in schöner Lage am IJ-Hafen und für den In- und Auslandsdienst in unmittelbarer Nähe des Hauptbahnhofs und ist mittels einer direkten Bahnverbindung - der "Schiphol-Linie" - auch mit Schiphol verbunden.
   Täglich verarbeitet der Postdienst der PTT viele Millionen Briefe und Pakete, größtenteils vollautomatisch.

Le centre d'expéditions des "PTT Post", bien situé au bord de l'IJ à Amsterdam et près de la Gare Centrale, ce qui favorise le trafic postal à l'intérieur, à l'extérieur, également par Schiphol, une liaison ferroviaire directe ("Schiphollijn") reliant la Gare et l'aéroport.
   Chaque jour ouvrable, le service des Postes des PTT traite - en grande partie de façon automatisée - des millions d'envois postaux.

El Centro de Distribución Postal de Amsterdam tiene una ubicación preciosa junto al puerto del IJ y, muy eficaz, cerca de la Estación Central, para la expedición postal nacional y extranjera, también vía Schiphol, por medio de una línea ferroviaria directa (la Línea Schiphol).
   Cada jornada laboral "PTT Post" tramita - en su mayor parte de forma automatizada - millones de cartas y paquetes.

　アムステルダムの郵便物区分所は、アイ港にあり、国内・国際郵便物を発送するのに便利なセントラル・ステーション付近です。またアムステルダム・セントラル・ステーションは、スキポール国際空港とも直通のスキポール線で結ばれています。
　毎日PTT（オランダ航空）では、数百万におよぶ手紙と小包を扱っています。

Amsterdam South-East, Complex of office buildings

'De Bullewijk', a former polder in the aerea, is presently notable for a huge complex of office blocks in the Amstel III industrial estate located in south east Amsterdam.

Many renowned companies, Dutch as well as foreign, have chosen this spot because of the good road links to near-by Schiphol airport and the parking facilities under the buildings.

"De Bullewijk", eens een polder in dit gebied, is tegenwoordig de aanduiding voor een enorm complex kantoorgebouwen op het Amstel III industrie-terrein, gelegen in Amsterdam Zuid-Oost.

Vele gerenommeerde bedrijven - Nederlandse, zowel als internationale - hebben deze plek gekozen, vanwege de verkeersfaciliteiten naar Schiphol en de parkeermogelijkheid onder de gebouwen.

"De Bullewijk", ein ehemaliges Marschland in diesem Gebiet, ist heute der Name für ein riesiges Konglomerat von Bürohäusern im Industriegebiet "Amstel III", im Südosten der Stadt.

Viele angesehene Unternehmen, sowohl niederländische als auch internationale, haben sich hier niedergelassen, und zwar wegen den Verbindungsmöglichkeiten mit Schiphol und den Parkmöglichkeiten unter den Gebäuden.

"De Bullewijk", ancien polder, est aujourd'hui le nom d'un grand complexe d'immeubles de bureaux dans la zone industrielle Amstel III, située dans la partie sud-est d'Amsterdam.

De nombreuses entreprises réputées, néerlandaises et internationales, ont choisi l'endroit à cause des facilités qu'offrent les routes vers Schiphol et des parkings spacieux sous les bâtiments.

"De Bullewijk", anteriormente un pólder de esta zona, es hoy en día la denominación de un enorme complejo de edificios de oficinas en la zona industrial Amstel III, situada en Amsterdam Sur-Este.

Muchas empresas renombradas - holandesas tanto como internacionales - han optado por este sitio, a causa de las facilidades de circulación hacia Schiphol y las posibilidades de aparcamiento bajo los edificios.

「デ・ブルワイク」はもとこの周辺の干拓地でしたが、現在はアムステルダムの東南にあるアムステル第三工業用地のオフィスビル街として重要となりました。

著名なオランダ及び外資大企業の多くが、この地を選んだ理由として、スキポール空港への交通の便が非常によいことと、大規模な地下駐車場が上げられます。

Naarden, Fortress

Spanish troops had long retreated when, in 1685 after ten years of building, the town had been recreated into a fortress. For the Peace Treaty of Munster ending 80 years of war with Spain was signed on January 30th 1648.

The Czech humanist and educationalist Jan Amos Comenius was buried within these town walls in 1670.

Toen in 1685, na tien jaar bouwen, de stad in een vesting was herschapen, waren de Spaanse troepen reeds lang vertrokken. Immers, de Vrede van Munster, die de 80-jarige oorlog met Spanje beëindigde, werd op 30 januari 1648 getekend.

De Tsjechische humanist en pedagoog Jan Amos Comenius werd in 1670 binnen deze stadsmuren begraven.

Als die Stadt im Jahre 1685 nach einer zehnjähriger Bautätigkeit zu einer Festung umgebaut worden war, hatten sich die spanischen Truppen schon lange zurückgezogen. Denn der Friede von Münster, der das Ende des 80 jährigen Krieges mit Spanien besiegelte, war ja bereits am 30. Januar 1648 geschlossen worden.

Der tschechische Humanist Johann Amos Comenius wurde 1670 innerhalb der Mauern dieser Stadt begraben.

Lorsqu'en 1685, après dix années de travaux, Naarden se fut transformée en une ville fortifiée, les troupes espagnoles étaient déjà parties depuis longtemps. C'est que le traité de Münster, qui mettait fin à la guerre avec l'Espagne, date du 30 janvier 1648.

Jan Amos Comenius, pédagogue et humaniste tchèque, fut enterré en 1670 à l'intérieur des murs.

En 1685, después de diez años de construcción, la ciudad fue convertida de nuevo en una fortaleza; las tropas españolas ya se habían marchado hacía tiempo, questo que la Paz de Westfalia, que puso fin a la guerra de Flandes con España, se firmó el 30 de enero de 1648.

El humanista y pedagogo checo Johann Amos Comenius fue enterrado dentro de estas murallas en 1670.

　10年の歳月をかけてナーデンの町を要塞として再築した1685年には、80年間にわたってオランダを占領していたスペイン群は、1648年1月30日に結ばれたムンスターの平和条約によって、とっくにオランダを引き上げていました。
　チェコスロバキア人の人道主義者で教育家であったヤン・アモス・コメニウスは、1670年に亡くなり、この町を包囲する壁の下に埋葬されました。

Hilversum, The Town Hall

The Town Hall of Hilversum is well known for its architecture by Willem Marinus Dudok and was built between 1928 and 1932.

Because of Hilversum's central location in the Netherlands, our broadcasting companies were founded here. In November 1919 the first news bulletins were being broadcast at regular times.

Het stadhuis van Hilversum is zeer bekend vanwege de architectuur door Willem Marinus Dudok en werd gebouwd van 1928-1932.

Vanwege de centrale ligging van Hilversum in Nederland, werd hier ons omroepbestel gevestigd. De eerste berichten gingen in november 1919 met vaste regelmaat de ether in.

Das Rathaus von Hilversum ist sehr bekannt wegen seiner Architektur, die auf Willem Marinus Dudok zurückgeht; es wurde von 1928 bis 1932 erbaut.

Wegen der Zentrallage von Hilversum ließ sich hier der niederländische Rundfunk nieder. Die ersten regelmäßigen Sendungen wurden im November 1919 ausgestrahlt.

La mairie de Hilversum, construite entre 1928 et 1932 par Willem Marinus Dudok, est d'un grand intérêt architectural.

Situé au centre du pays, Hilversum se prêtait bien à recevoir les stations de radiodiffusion et de télévision nationales. Depuis novembre 1919, les premières nouvelles ont été diffusées régulièrement.

El Ayuntamiento de Hilversum es muy famoso por la arquitectura de Willem Marinus Dudok y fue construido de 1928 a 1932.

A causa de la situación central que ocupa Hilversum de los Países Bajos, se fundaron aquí las cadenas nacionales de radiodifusión. Las primeras noticias empezaron a trasmitirse con regularidad en noviembre de 1919.

ヒルバーサムの市庁舎は、有名な建築家ヴィルム・マリウス・デュードックの設計により、1928年から1932年にかけて建設されました。

オランダの真ん中にあるという地理的条件により、ここには放送局が密集しています。最初の定期ニュース放送は、1919年11月に開始されました。

Haarlem, Capital of the province of North Holland

From a small, 11th century settlement on the banks of the river Spaarne Haarlem developed into a flourishing city. The capital of the province of North Holland received municipal rights in 1245.

The history of the development of printing is housed in the museum Joh. Enschedé & Zoon at Klokhuis square.

Van een kleine nederzetting aan het Spaarne uit de 11e eeuw, groeide Haarlem uit tot een bloeiende stad. De hoofdstad van de provincie Noord-Holland verkreeg stadsrechten in 1245.

De geschiedenis van de ontwikkeling der boekdrukkunst is ondergebracht in het museum Joh. Enschedé & Zoon aan het Klokhuisplein.

Haarlem entwickelte sich im 11. Jahrhundert von einer kleinen Siedlung am Ufer der Spaarne zu einer blühenden Stadt. Das Stadtrecht wurde der Hauptstadt der Provinz Nord-Holland im Jahre 1245 verliehen.

Der historischen Entwicklung der Buchdruckerkunst ist das Museum Joh. Enschedé & Zoon am Klokhuisplein gewidmet.

Au XIe s. petite colonie de peuplement au bord de la Spaarne, Haarlem, de nos jours, est devenue une ville florissante. Cheflieu de la province de la Hollande-Septentrionale, elle obtint en 1245 les privilèges communaux.

La collection du Musée Joh. Enschedé & Zoon, situé Klokhuisplein, est consacrée à l'histoire du développement de l'imprimerie.

Haarlem se convirtió de un pequeño asentamiento del siglo XI situado a orillas del río Spaarne, en una ciudad floreciente. La capital de la provincia de Holanda del Norte consiguió derechos municipales en 1245.

La historia del desarrollo de la imprenta está albergada en el museo Joh. Enschedé & Zoon en la plaza llamada Klokhuis.

11世紀にスパーン川沿いの小さな部落として生まれたハーレムは、繁栄をきわめた市と成長しました。北ホーランド州の州都であるこの市は、すでに1245年に町としての自治権を得ることができました。

クロックハウス広場にあるヨハン・エンスヘーデ博物館は、印刷技術発展の歴史博物館です。

Velsen,
Tunnel crossing the North Sea Canal

Work on the 'Velsertunnel' began in 1941 but was halted a year later by the occupying forces.
A new start was made in 1952 and both the railway and car tunnel were officially opened in 1957.

Na in 1941 te zijn begonnen, werden de werkzaamheden aan de Velsertunnel een jaar later op last van de bezetter gestaakt.
Een nieuw begin werd gemaakt in 1952 en zowel de spoor- als autotunnel werden in 1957 officieel geopend.

1941 wurde mit dem Bau des Velsertunnels begonnen. Ein Jahr später aber wurden die Bauarbeiten auf Befehl der Besatzungsmacht eingestellt.
1952 wurde ein Neuanfang gemacht, und im Jahr 1957 wurden sowohl der Eisenbahn- als auch der Verkehrstunnel offiziell eröffnet.

Les travaux du "Velsertunnel", commencés en 1941, furent arrêtés un an après, sur décision de l'occupant.
Les travaux ayant été repris en 1952, le tunnel de chemin de fer et le tunnel routier furent ouverts officiellement en 1957.

Habiéndose dado comienzo a la construcción del "Velsertunnel" en 1941, se cesó de trabajar en este túnel un año más tarde por orden de las fuerzas ocupadoras.
Se comenzó de nuevo en 1952 y tanto el túnel ferroviario como el túnel para coches fueron inaugurados oficialmente en 1957.

1941年に建設開始をしてから1年後に、ドイツ占領軍はフェルセー・トンネルの建設にストップをかけました。
1952年に新スタートをきり、1957年には鉄道と自動車用の両トンネルが正式に開通しました。

(Overleaf) IJmuiden, Piers and Blast Furnaces

IJmuiden was once a quaint fishing village on the Nort Sea coast. Since the port of Amsterdam needed a shorter route to the sea it was decided to dig a canal of 24 kilometers in length through the dunes from IJmuiden to Amsterdam. After the opening of the Nort Sea Canal on November 1st 1876 a prosperous industry grew on the north bank in Velsen. The steel industry embodied in the Blast Furnace complex is presently the centre.

IJmuiden was eens een pittoresk vissersplaatsje aan de Noordzeekust. Aangezien echter de haven van Amsterdam dringend behoefte had aan een kortere route naar zee, werd besloten een kanaal van 24 kilometer lengte te graven door de duinen van IJmuiden naar Amsterdam. Na de opening van het Noordzeekanaal op 1 november 1876, ontstond op de Noordelijke oever in Velsen een bloeiende industrie, waarvan de staalindustrie, belichaamd in het huidige Hoogoven-complex, thans het middelpunt vormt.

IJmuiden war einstmals ein malerisches Fisherdorf an der Nordseeküste. Als man für den Amsterdamer Hafen aber eines kürzeren Weges zum Meer bedurfte, wurde ein Kanal mit einer Länge von 24 Kilometern durch die Dünen von IJmuiden nach Amsterdam angelegt. Nach der Eröffnung des Nordsee-Kanals am 1. November 1876 entstand am nördlichen Ufer von Velsen allmählich eine blühende Industrie, deren Mittelpunkt heute das Hüttenwerk von Hoogoven ist.

A l'origine IJmuiden était un petit port de pêche sur la côte de la mer du Nord. Comme le port d'Amsterdam avait intérêt à la construction d'un canal qui le relierait à la mer, on a décidé de construire le Canal de la mer du Nord, 24 kilomètres de long, à travers les dunes d'IJmuiden à Amsterdam. Après l'ouverture du canal, le 1er novembre 1876, une industrie s'est développée au nord, à Velsen, dont la métallurgie constitue, aujourd'hui, l'élément principal, incarné dans le complexe des hautsfournaux.

Antiguamente IJmuiden ere un pintoresco pueblo de pescadores situado en la costa del Mar del Norte. Sin embargo, ya que el puerto de Amsterdam necesitaba urgentemente una ruta más corta al mar, se decidió cavar un canal de 24 kilómetros de longitud a través de las dunas, desde IJmuiden hasta Amsterdam. Después de la inauguración del Canal del Mar del Norte el 1 de noviembre de 1876, surgió en Velsen, en la orilla norte, una industria próspera cuyo núcleo lo forma la industria del acero, representada en el actual complejo de Altos Hornos.

　昔アイマウデンは北海に面した古めかしい漁村でした。けれどアムステルダム港が海への短いルートを必要とするにあたって、アイマウデンからアムステルダムまで24キロの砂丘をぬける運河が建設されることになりました。1876年11月1日に北海運河が開通されると、フェルセンの北岸に工業が栄えるようになり、現在では熔鉱炉が立ち並ぶ製鉄業が中心となっています。

Zandvoort, Colourful beetles in the sand

All bounds are literally exceeded when the first rays of the sun descent on the coastline of the Low Lands. The sun-loving Dutch, with many foreign tourists in their wake, take off for the beach of Zandvoort.

Their enthusiasm is has high as the tide and like colourful beetles they nestle down in the sand to bask in the warmth of the sun.

Alle grenzen worden letterlijk overschreden, wanneer de eerste zonnestralen op Neerlands' kust neerdalen. De Nederlandse zonaanbidders, met in hun kielzog vele buitenlandse toeristen, begeven zich dan naar het strand van Zandvoort.

Daar viert hun enthousiasme hoogtij - ook bij eb - en als kleurige kevertjes vleien zij zich in het zand om zich te laten koesteren door de zonnewarmte.

Ein wahrhaft grenzüberschreitendes Erlebnis! Wenn die holländischen Küsten im ersten Sonnenlicht erstrahlen, ziehen die niederländischen Sonnenanbeter zum Strand in Zandvoort - und mit ihnen die vielen Scharen ausländischer Touristen.

Dort kennt ihre Begeisterung keine Grenzen, und wie bunte Käfer schmiegen sie sich in den Sand, um sich von der Sonne wärmen zu lassen.

Toutes les frontières sont franchies, au sens propre, quand les premiers rayons de soleil descendent sur la côte hollandaise. Les adorateurs du soleil néerlandais et les touristes étrangers qui suivent leur sillage se rendent à la plage de Zandvoort.

Leur enthousiasme y fleurit et comme des escarbots colorés ils s'étendent sur le sable pour lézarder au soleil.

En cuanto los primeros rayos de sol descienden sobre el litoral neerlandés se desbordan literalmente todos los límites. Los amantes del sol holandeses se dirigen a la playa de Zandvoort, imitados por muchos turistas extranjeros.

Su entusiasmo es desbordante como la marea más alta - incluso con marea baja - y como escarabajos de tonos vivos se acomodan en la arena para dejarse acariciar por el calor del sol.

太陽の光線がオランダの海岸を覆うようになってくると、誰でも気が浮き立ってきます。太陽崇拝者であるオランダ人は、数多くの外国人観光客にまじって、ザンドフォートの海岸にでむかいます。

満ち潮のように昂揚した気分で、太陽のあたたかさをエンジョイするため、それぞれ色とりどりの水着で身を砂の上に横たえます。

Alkmaar, Famous cheese town

As the aerial photograph clearly shows Alkmaar is really a magnificent fortress.

Naturally, the town, which received municipal rights in 1254, is world famous for its cheese market, held every Friday morning from April until October. Nowadays a folk spectacle, particularly for the many tourists, it has been the sight for serious cheese trading for centuries.

Zoals de luchtfoto duidelijk laat zien, is Alkmaar eigenlijk een prachtige vestingstad.

Uiteraard is de gemeente - die stadsrechten verwierf in 1254 - wereldbekend om de kaasmarkt, die iedere vrijdagmorgen van april tot oktober wordt gehouden. Tegenwoordig een folkloristisch schouwspel voor met name de vele toeristen, vond er eeuwenlang een serieuze kaashandel plaats.

Aus dem Luftbild erhellt, daß Alkmaar im Grunde genommen eine prächtige Festungsstadt ist.

Die Stadt, der im Jarhe 1254 Stadtrechte verliehen wurden, ist wegen ihres Käsemarktes, der jeden Freitagmorgen von April bis Oktober abgehalten wird, weltberühmt. Obgleich der Markt über viele Jahrhunderte dem Käsehandel diente, stellt er heutzutage ein folkloristisches Schauspiel für die vielen Touristen dar.

La photo nous montre nettement qu'au fond Alkmaar est une ville fortifiée magnifique. Elle obtint ses privilèges communaux en 1254.

Réputé pour son marché des fromages, Alkmaar offre aux multiples touristes - tous les vendredis matin du mois d'avril jusqu'au mois d'octobre - un spectacle folklorique, le commerce des fromages, qui existe déjà depuis des siècles.

Como se aprecia claramente en la fotografía aérea, Alkmaar es en realidad una magnífica fortaleza.

Naturalmente que la ciudad - que consiguió derechos municipales en 1254 - tiene renombre mundial por su mercado de queso, que se celebra todos los viernes por la mañana de abril a octubre. Hoy en día es un espectáculo folkórico, particularmente para los muchos turistas; aquí es donde durante siglos ha tenido lugar el serio comercio de queso.

この航空写真が示すように、アルカマーは実際は完璧な要塞なのです。

しかし1254年に自治権を得たアルカマーの町は、4月から10月の毎金曜日の朝開かれるチーズ市場で世界的に有名です。今日このチーズ市場は、主に観光客向けの民族催物となっていますが、この地は数世紀にわたってチーズ貿易の中心地でした。

Schermerhorn, Windmills in the snow

These age-old windmills near Schermerhorn, covered with fresh snow, are a picture of romance and nostalgia.

The rest of the world has changed considerably, but it is to be hoped that these mills will turn their sails in the wind for centuries to come, to be enjoyed by posterity.

Deze eeuwenoude molens bij Schermerhorn, bestoven door verse sneeuw, vormen een beeld van romantiek en nostalgie.

De wereld er omheen is veel veranderd, maar het is te hopen dat deze molens nog eeuwen lang hun wieken in de wind zullen laten gaan, zodat het nageslacht ervan kan blijven genieten.

Eine romantische und nostalgische Szene: die mit frishem Schnee beschneiten, jahrhundertealten Mühlen bei Schermerhorn.

Zwar hat die Welt sich sehr verändert; man kann aber nur hoffen, daß die Flügel dieser Mühlen sich noch jahrhundertelang im Wind drehen werden, so daß die Nachwelt sich noch lange an ihrem Anblick erfreuen kann.

Les très vieux moulins près de Schermerhorn poudrés de neige fraîche évoquent une image de romantisme et de nostalgie.

Ses environs ont subi de profonds changements, mais espérons que les ailes du moulin à vent tourneront encore pendant des siècles pour que même la postérité en puisse jouir.

Estos molinos centenarios cerca de Schermerhorn, cubiertos de nieve fresca, crean una imagen de romanticismo y nostalgia.

El mundo que los rodea ha cambiado mucho, pero es de esperar que estos molinos hagan girar sus aspas al viento durante muchos siglos más, de forma que la posteridad pueda seguir disfrutando de ellos.

新雪に覆われたスヘルマーホーンの由緒ある風車は、ロマンチックでノスタルジアそのものです。

周囲の世界は変わりましたが、これから何世紀にもわたって、オランダの風車の翼はまわり続け、子孫の目を楽しませてもらいたいものです。

46

The 'Hondsbossche' Sea-wall

Following the St. Elizabeth flood in 1421 a sea wall was built between Camperduin and Petten. The formal tidal inlet 'de Zijpe' was therefore closed off and a dyke complex was built along a stretch of 5 km. The present dykes date back to 1870 and are called the 'Hondsbossche Zeewering'.

The dyke measures 75 meters at the foot and is more than 10 metres wide at the crown.

Na de St. Elizabethsvloed van 1421 werd een zeewering aangelegd tussen Camperduin en Petten. Het vroegere zeegat "de Zijpe" werd hierdoor afgesloten en over 5 kilometer lengte werd een dijken-complex aangelegd. Het huidige dijkenstelsel dateert uit 1870 en is bekend als de "Hondsbossche Zeewering".

Onderaan is de dijk 75 meter - en op de kruin ruim 10 meter breed.

Nach der St. Elisabeth-Flutkatastrophe im Jahre 1421 wurden zwischen Camperduin und Petten eine Küstenbefestigung angelegt. "De Zijpe", der ehemalige Zugang zum Meer, wurde dadurch vom Meer aberiegelt und über eine Länge von fünf Kilometern wurden Deiche angelegt. Die heutigen Deichanlagen stammen aus 1870 und sind unter dem Namen "Hondsbossche Zeewering" bekannt.

An seiner Sohle ist der Deich 75 und an seiner Kappe mehr als 10 Meter breit.

A la suite des terribles inondations dites de sainte Elisabeth en 1421, on entreprit la construction d'une dique de mer de cinq kilomètres entre Camperduin et Petten, qui fermait le chenal "de Zijpe". L'ensemble des diques actuel, dit le "Hondsbossche Zeewering", date de 1870.

Au pied la digue a 75 m. de large et au sommet plus de 10 m.

Después de haberse producido, en 1421, la inundación llamada de Santa Elisabet, se construyó un dique entre Camperduin y Petten. Con cello se cerró el que fue canal "de Zijpe" y se levantó todo un complejo de diques sobre una longitud de 5 kilómetros. El actual sistema de diques data de 1870 y se conoce por el nombre de "Hondsbossche Zeewering".

La parte inferior del dique tiene una anchura de 75 metros; la parte superior, más de 10 metros.

1421年のセント・エリザベス洪水の後、カンパーダウンとペッテンの間に海壁が建設されました。デ・ザイプと呼ばれていた以前の海口は閉めきれられ、5キロの堤防（ダイク）が造られました。現在の堤防は1870年からのもので、ホンズボッス海壁として知られています。

この堤防の幅は、下の部分が75メートル、上は10メートルです。

Bulbfields near Breezand

In the north of the province of North Holland, near the village of Breezand, the fields in spring display a multitude of colour. After waiting all winter under the soil the bulbs welcome the warmth and begin to flower.

For weeks a feast for the eyes, the bulbs are lifted to be replanted in the autumn.

In de kop van Noord-Holland, vlak bij het dorpje Breezand, veranderen de velden in het voorjaar tot een veelvoud van kleuren. Na de gehele winter in de grond te hebben gewacht op hogere temperaturen, komen de bollen tot bloei.

Wekenlang een lust voor het oog, worden zij gerooid om in het najaar weer de grond in te gaan.

Im nördlichen Teil Nordhollands, nahe dem Dorf Breezand, erstrahlen die Felder jesdes Frühjahr in voller Farbenpracht. Die Blumenzwiebeln haben den Winter über im Boden ausgeharrt und erblühen, sobald die Temperaturen im Frühjahr ansteigen.

Wochenlang sind sie eine Augenweide; schließlich gräbt man sie auf, um sie im Herbst wiederum in die Erde zu setzen.

Les champs près du village de Breezand, dans la partie nord de la Hollande-Septentrionale, se transforment, au printemps, en une débauche de couleurs. Les bulbes fleurissent, après un long hiver d'attente.

Régal pour les yeux pendant de longues semaines, elles seront arrachées pour être plantées à nouveau en automne.

En el extremo norte de la provincia de Holanda del Norte, cerca de la localidad de Breezand, los campos se convierten en primavera en multitud de colores. Después de haber esperado todo el invierno en la tierra temperaturas más altas, los bulbos florecen.

Durante muchas semanas recrean la vista y son luego arrancados para volver a plantarlos en otoño.

北ホーランド州の北部、ブレーザント村の付近は、春になると色の洪水の畑となります。長い冬辛抱強く土の中で、外があたたかくなるのを待っていた球根は、いっせいに花咲きます。

数週間にわたって皆の目を奪うと、球根は掘り出され、秋になってから再び土の中に戻されます。

Texel Island, from 7.000 feet

This aerial photograph taken at 7.000 ft. and by Dutch standards in extremely clear weather gives a spectacular view of the entire island of Texel. It belongs to the Wadden Shallow group. Part of the mainland a few thousand years ago, it is now divided by the Marsdiep.
   Texel is an outstanding holiday isle with delightful hamlets and villages and Den Burg as the capital. An enormous variety of birds use the island as a breeding ground.

Deze luchtopname, gemaakt vanaf een hoogte van 7.000 voet en bij - voor Nederlandse begrippen - uitzonderlijk helder weer, geeft een spectaculair beeld van het gehele Waddeneiland Texel. Vóór onze jaartelling nog een deel van het vasteland, is het nu daarvan gescheiden door het Marsdiep.
   Texel is een vakantiebestemming bij uitstek. Er zijn verschillende mooie buurtschappen en dorpen, met als hoofdplaats Den Burg. Een grote variatie vogels gebruikt het eiland als broedplaats.

Dieses Luftbild, das in einer Höhe von 7000 Fuß und bei für niederländische Verhältnisse außerordentlich klarem Wetter entstand, ist eine geradezu spektakuläre Aufnahme der gesamten Watteninsel Texel. Vor der Zeitwende war die Insel noch Teil des Festlandes. Jetzt trennt das "Marsdiep" die Insel vom Land.
   Texel ist der Ferienort schlechthin. Es gibt dort mehrere schöne Weiler und Dörfchen. Wichtigster Ort ist Den Burg. Die Insel ist Brutstätte für viele Vogelarten.

Cette photographie aérienne prise d'une altitude de 7000 pieds et par un ciel extrêmement clair - ce qui est assez rare en Hollande - donne une image spectaculaire de l'île des Wadden Texel. Avant notre ère, elle faisait encore partie du continent; de nos jours elle en est séparée par le "Marsdiep".
   Destination pour les vacances par excellence, elle offre plusieurs hameaux et villages attrayants et son chef-lieu Den Burg. Une grande variété d'oiseaux y couvent.

Esta fotografía aèrea, hecha desde una altura de 7.000 pies y en un día - para el criterio holandés - excepcionalmente claro, ofrece una imagen espectacular de toda la isla frisona de Texel. Antes de la era cristiana formaba todavía parte de la tierra firme, pero actualmente queda separada de ella por la vía fluvial Marsdiep.
   Texel es un lugar de vacaciones por excelencia. Hay bonitas aldeas y pueblos, de los que Den Burg es el más importante. La isla sirve de criadero a una gran variedad de pájaros.

　　このオランダにとっては非常に晴天という日に、約2000メートルの上空から撮影された航空写真は、ワッダン浅瀬群島のテッセル島全体のすばらしい姿を表しています。今世紀前までは本土につながっていましたが、現在ではマースディップがこの島と本土を分けています。
　　テッセル島は、最高のリゾート地です。この島は幾つかの美しい小村落からなっており、そのうちデン・ブルグが首村です。この島は、多種の鳥の繁殖地です。

The Zuider Zee Dam, 'Afsluitdijk'

The construction of the Afsluitdijk, a large sea dam between the former Zuiderzee and the Wadden Sea, was begun in 1923 and completed in 1932.

The dyke, comprising five drain locks, runs for a total of 32.5 km. A road runs along the dyke, the E10 motorway, forming part of the European motorway system.

Met de bouw van de Afsluitdijk - in feite een zware zeedam tussen de voormalige Zuiderzee en de Waddenzee - werd in 1923 begonnen en het geheel werd voltooid in 1932.

De dijk, waarin vijf uitwaterende sluizen zijn gebouwd is in totaal 32,5 kilometer lang. Over de dijk loopt een weg, die als de E10 deel uitmaakt van het Europese wegennet.

Mit dem Bau des Abschlußdeichs - eigentlich ein schwerer Seedeich zwischen der ehemaligen Zuidersee und dem Wattenmeer - wurde 1923 begonnen. 1932 wurde der Bau vollendet.

Der Deich, in den fünf Ablaßschleusen eingebaut wurden, ist insgesamt 32,5 Kilometer lang. Über den Deich läuft eine Straße, die dem europäischen Straßennetz als E10 angehört.

La construction de la Digue de Nord - grande digue de clôture entre l'ancien Zuiderzee et la Waddenzee - commencée en 1923 fut achevée en 1932.

La digue, qui compte cinq écluses d'évacuation, a une longueur de 32,5 kilomètres. Sur la digue, une route, la E 10, qui fait partie du réseau routier européen.

En 1923 se dió comienzo a la construcción del dique de cierre ''Afsluitdijk'' - de hecho un dique pesado marino entre el que fue al Mar Zuiderzee y el Mar Frisón - y en 1932 era una realidad.

El dique, en el que están construidas cinco esclusas de desagüe, tiene en total 32,5 kilómetros de longitud. Sobre él pasa una carretera, la E10, que forma parte de la red europea de carreteras.

締切り堤防は、以前のザウダー海とワッダン海の間に建設された、おおがかりな海洋ダムです。1923年に工事が開始され、完成されたのは1932年でした。

この全長32.5キロの堤防には、排水用の水門が5か所あり、ヨーロッパ道路網の一環をなすハイウェイ E10 が堤防の上を通っています。

West-Terschelling, Harbour

The Wadden island of Terschelling, like Ameland a municipality belonging to the province of Friesland, is 28 km in length and 2 to 5 km wide.

Ferry boats constantly sail in and out of the harbour carrying particularly in summer large numbers of Dutch and foreign tourists.

Het Waddeneiland Terschelling, net als Ameland een gemeente behorende tot de provincie Friesland, is 28 kilometer lang en van 2 tot 5 kilometer breed.

In de haven van West-Terschelling is het een constant komen en gaan van veerboten om - vooral in het zomerseizoen - de vele Nederlandse en buitenlandse toeristen te vervoeren.

Die Watteninsel Terschelling ist 28 Kilometer lang und 2 bis 5 Kilometer breit und gehört wie die Insel Ameland zur Provinz Friesland.

Im Hafen von West-Terschelling laufen die Fähren ein und aus; diese befördern insbesondere während der Sommersaison die vielen niederländischen und ausländischen Touristen.

L'île des Wadden Terschelling faisant partie de la province de Frise, tout comme l'île d'Ameland, a 28 kilomètres de long sur 2 à 5 kilomètres de large.

Remarquez le va-et-vient ininterrompu des bacs dans le port de West-Terschelling. En été surtout, ils transportent un grand nombre de touristes néerlandais et étrangers.

La isla frisona de Terschelling, al igual que Ameland un municipio perteneciente a la provincia de Frisia, tiene una longitud de 28 kilómetros y una anchura de 2 a 5 kilómetros.

En el puerto de West-Terschelling, en el oeste de la isla, hay un constante ir y venir de transbordadores que - sobre todo en la temporada de verano - transportan a los muchos turistas holandeses y extranjeros.

ワッダン群島のテスヘリング島は、アーメランド島と同じようにフリースランド州内にあり、長さ28キロ、幅は2キロから5キロです。

特に夏のシーズン中には、西テスヘリングの港には、オランダ国内そして海外からの観光客を運ぶフェリー船が、頻繁に行き通います。

Ameland, Hollum

This aerial view taken above the Wadden island Ameland shows an attractive piece of the North coast. At low tide it is possible to walk from the Frisian coast to Ameland and back. Traversing these mud flats by foot is an activity which has gained international fame. The municipality consists of four main centres: Nes, which is the main town, Hollum (see aerial view), Ballum and Buren. The major source of income is tourism due to the island's 20 km of coastline.

Van het Waddeneiland Ameland laat deze luchtopname een mooi stukje Noordkust zien. Bij eb kan men te voet van de Friese kust naar Ameland gaan en vice versa. Het "wadlopen" is internationaal populair. De gemeente bestaat uit vier kernen: de hoofdplaats Nes, Hollum (te zien op de luchtfoto), Ballum en Buren. De belangrijkste bron van bestaan is het toerisme, vanwege de kuststrook van 20 km lengte.

Diese Luftaufnahme zeigt einen schönen Ausschnitt der Nordküste der Watteninsel Ameland. Bei Ebbe gelangt man zu Fuß von der friesischen Küste nach Ameland und wieder zurück. Wattwanderungen sind allgemein beliebt. Die Gemeinde setzt sich aus vier Kernen zusammen. Die wichtigsten Orte sind Nes, Hollum (auf dem Bild zu erkennen), Ballum und Buren. Es nimmt nicht Wunder, daß mit einer 20 Kilometer langen Küste der Tourismus die wichtigste Erwerbsquelle ist.

La photo nous montre une belle partie de la côte du nord de l'île des Wadden Ameland. La marée basse permet de traverser à gué les Wadden - activité populaire dans de nombreux pays - depuis la côte frisonne jusqu'à l'île d'Ameland et vice-versa. La commune se compose de quatre centres: le chef-lieu Nes, Hollum, qu'on voit nettement sur la photo, Ballum et Buren. Source de revenus principale: les touristes attirés par le long littoral (20 km.).

Esta fotografía aérea muestra una bonita parte de la costa norte de la isla frisona de Ameland. Cuando hay marea baja se puede ir a pie de la costa de Frisia a Ameland y viceversa. El andar por las marismas ha obtenido popularidad internacional. El municipio está compuesto de cuatro núcleos: la capital Nes, Hollum (que se puede ver en la fotografía), Ballum y Buren. La principal fuente de ingresos es el turismo, gracias a la franja costera de 20 km de longitud.

　この航空写真には、ワッダン群島のアーメランド島の美しい北側の海岸の一部が写っています。干潮時には、フリースランドの本土からアーメランド島まで歩いて渡ることができます。これは「ワッダン・ハイキング」（ワッダン・ローパン）と呼ばれて、国際的にポピュラーなレジャースポーツです。この島には、ネス、ホーラム（この航空写真に写っている村）、バーレムとビューレンの主なる四村があります。アーメランドの最も重要な収入源は、20キロにわたる海岸線を利用した観光業です。

Leeuwarden, Capital of the province of Friesland

Leeuwarden grew from three knoll villages. In 1435 the districts of Nijenhove, Oldehove and Hoek were extended and fell inside the city boundary.

The world famous spy Mata Hari (Malaysian for 'Eye of the Day') was born in Leeuwarden in 1876. Her real name was Margaretha Geertruida Zella. She married an army captain and in 1895 left for the Dutch Indies.

Leeuwarden is ontstaan uit drie terpendorpen. In 1435 werden de stadsgebieden Nijenhove, Oldehove en Hoek uitgebreid, waarna het geheel binnen de omwalling kwam te liggen.

De wereldbekende spionne ''Mata Hari'' (Maleis voor ''Oog van de Dag'') werd in 1876 in Leeuwarden geboren als Margaretha Geertruida Zelle. Zij trouwde een legerkapitein en vertrok in 1895 naar Ned. Indië.

Leeuwarden entstand aus drei Wurtensiedlungen. Im Jahre 1435 wurden die Stadtbezirke Nijenhove, Oldehove und Hoek erweitert, und anschließend wurden das Ganze mit einem Wall umgeben.

Die berühmte Spionin ''Mata Hari''- ''Des Tages Auge'' in Malaysischen - wurde als Margaretha Geertruida Zelle 1876 in Leeuwarden geboren. Sie heiratete einen Hauptmann und fuhr 1895 nach Niederländisch-Ostindien.

Trois tertres sont à l'origine de Leeuwarden. En 1435, les quartiers Nijenhove, Oldehove et Hoek ont été agrandis. Ils étaient alors, tous les trois, entourés de murailles.

Mata-Hari - malais pour ''Oeil du Jour'' - (Margaretha Geertruida Zelle, dite), espionne connue dans le monde entier, naquit en 1876 à Leeuwarden. Epouse d'un capitaine de l'armée hollandaise, elle partit en 1895 en Indonésie.

Leeuwarden tiene su origen en tres pueblos terpe (construidos sobre una colina artificial, contra inundaciones). En 1435 se ensancharon los límites municipales de Nijenhove, Oldehove y Hoek, por lo que el conjunto llegó a situarse dentro de las murallas.

La mundialmente famosa espía ''Mata Hari'' (en malayo, 'el Ojo del Día') nació en Leeuwarden en 1876 como Margaretha Geertruida Zelle. Se casó con un capitán del ejército y se marchó a las Indias holandesas en 1895.

レウワーデン市の起源は、三村の小丘の村落でした。1435年にはナイエンホーバ、オルデホーバとフックが拡張され、この全体の周囲に壁がめぐらされました。

世界的に有名なスパイ、マタ・ハリ（マレー語で「日の目」という意味）は1876年にマーガレッタ・ヘートラウダ・ゼレとしてレウワーデンに生まれました。陸軍大尉と結婚してから、マタ・ハリは1895年にインドネシアに移り住みました。

Sneek, During national ice-skating event

This picturesque view of Sneek was taken during the biggest national ice skating event 'The Eleven Towns Skating Race'. The first race was held on January 2nd 1909. The eleven Frisian towns along the route are Leeuwarden, Dokkum, Franeker, Harlingen, Bolsward, Workum, Hindelopen, Staveren, Sloten, IJlst and Sneek. The photograph shows the public on the ice near the water gate, built in 1613.

Deze schilderachtige opname van Sneek werd gemaakt tijdens het grootste nationale schaatsfestijn "De Elfstedentocht". Op 2 januari 1909 werd de eerste tocht, waarbij elf Friese steden moeten worden aangedaan, verreden. Deze elf steden zijn: Leeuwarden, Dokkum, Franeker, Harlingen, Bolsward, Workum, Hindelopen, Staveren, Sloten, IJlst en Sneek. De luchtfoto toont het publiek op het ijs nabij de waterpoort, daterend uit 1613.

Diese malerische Aufnahme von Sneek entstand während der größten nationalen Eislaufveranstaltung, des sogenannten "Elf-Städte-Laufs". Am 2. Januar 1909 wurde der erste Lauf entlang den elf friesischen Städten ausgetragen; bei den elf Städten handelt es sich um: Leeuwarden, Dokkum, Franeker, Harlingen, Bolsward, Workum, Hindelopen, Staveren, Sloten, IJlst und Sneek. Diese Luftbild zeigt die Zuschauer auf dem Eis nahe einem aus dem Jahre 1613 stammenden Wassertor.

Cette photo pittoresque de Sneek fut prise pendant le grand festin national de patinage "le circuit des onze villes". La première course passant par onze villes de Frise eut lieu le 2 janvier 1909. Les villes: Leeuwarden, Dokkum, Franeker, Harlingen, Bolsward, Workum, Hindelopen, Staveren, Sloten, IJlst et Sneek. La photo nous montre le public sur la glace près de la poterne datant de 1613.

Esta pintoresca fotografía de Sneek fue sacada durante el mayor espectáculo nacional de patinaje, la vuelta a las once ciudades: "Elfstedentocht". El 2 de enero de 1909 se corrió la primera vuelta, en la que se tiene que pasar por once ciudades frisonas, a saber: Leeuwarden, Dokkum, Franeker, Harlingen, Bolsward, Workum, Hindelopen, Staveren, Sloten, IJlst y Sneek. La fotografía aérea muestra al público divirtiéndose en el hielo cerca de la 'puerta del agua', del año 1613.

　絵に描いたようなこのスネークの写真は、全国から参加者が集まるスケート大会「11都市ツワー」の時に撮影されたものです。1909年1月2日に初めて、フリースランドの11都市をスケートでツワーする催しが行われました。これらの11都市とは、レウワーデン、ドッカム、フラネカー、ハーリンヘン、ボルスワード、ウォーカム、ヒインダーローペン、スターヴェレン、スローテン、アイルストとスネークです。この航空写真は、1613年に建設された水門付近の氷上の人々を示しています。

Burum, Satellite Groundstation

The Dutch satellite ground station at Burum. Virtually all satellite activities take place in this rural location in the province of Friesland, free from transmitter network interference.

Eight dish antennae of various sizes are aimed at satellites circling the earth in geostationary orbit providing rapid and efficient world-wide telecommunications.

Het Nederlandse satellietgrondstation te Burum. Vanuit deze landelijke lokatie in de provincie Friesland, vrij van storende invloeden van het straalzendernet, vindt vrijwel al het satellietverkeer plaats.

Acht schotelantennes van verschillende afmetingen staan gericht op satellieten, die in een geostationaire baan om de aarde cirkelen. Zo is een snelle transmissie mogelijk van telefoonverkeer, dataverkeer en televisiebeelden van en naar alle delen van de wereld.

Die niederländische Satelliten-Bodenstation in Burum. Von diesem ländlichen, ''störungsfreien'' Gelände in der Provinz Friesland aus findet nahezu der gesamte Satellitenfunk statt.

Acht Parabolantennen unterschiedlicher Maße stehen in Verbindung mit Satelliten, die die Erde in einer geostationären Umlaufbahn umkreisen. Dies ermöglicht eine schnelle Übertragung und Empfang des Sprech- und Datenverkehrs und von Fernsehbildern in und aus aller Welt.

La géostation de satellites à Burum. C'est ici, dans la campagne frisonne, qu'on contrôle - sans perturbations des relais hertziens - presque toutes les communications par satellite.

Huit antennes paraboliques de dimensions différentes sont orientées vers des satellites gravitant sur une orbite géostationnaire autour de notre planète. Elles permettent une transmission rapide de communications téléphoniques, de données informatiques et de programmes de télévision aux quatre coins du monde.

La estación de tierra holandesa para la emisión de satélites, en Burum. Desde esta ubicación rural en la provincia de Frisia, libre de interferencias de la red de emisoras radiales, se efectúa casi toda la comunicación por satélite.

Ocho antenas platillo de diferentes tamaños están apuntando a satélites que dan vueltas a la tierra en una órbita geoestacionaria, lo que permite una rápida transmisión de comunicación telefónica, datos e imágenes de televisión desde y hacia todas las partes del mundo.

ビューラムのオランダ衛星地上基地。フリースランドの牧歌的な風景が背景のこの場所には、電波を妨げる影響が少なく、衛星通信のほとんどがここで行われます。八の大小の円形アンテナは、相対同位置を保ちながら地球を巡る衛星に向けられています。このような通信衛星によって、世界各国からの電話やデータの、迅速な通信が可能となるのです。

A true Frisian happening: 'Skûtsjesilen'

Friesland's abundant lakes encourage sailing. The major annual event, particularly for the Frisians, is 'skûtsjesilen'. Professional sailors compete in tjalks before the eyes of fellow boat lovers who arrive in large numbers from Friesland, the rest of the Netherlands as well as abroad. They come to the Frisian lakes in their own boats to have a closer view of the spectacle.

Vanwege de vele meren in Friesland, wordt er veel aan zeilsport gedaan. Hét jaarlijkse evenement vooral voor de Friese watersportliefhebbers is het "skûtsjesilen", waaraan wordt deelgenomen door zeiltjalken met beroepsschippers. Veel toeschouwers uit Friesland, Nederland en ook het buitenland komen in hun bootjes naar de Friese meren om het schouwspel van dichtbij gade te kunnen slaan.

Friesland mit seinen vielen Meeren eignet sich vorzüglich für den Wassersport. Die größte Veranstaltung, insbesondere für die friesischen Wassersportfreunde, ist das "Skûtsjesilen", an dem sich Segeltjalken mit Berufsschiffer beteiligen. Viele Zuschauer aus Friesland, den Niederlanden, aber auch aus dem Ausland begeben sich mit ihrem Booten zu den Friesischen Meeren, um sich dieses Schauspiel aus nächster Nähe anzusehen.

La voile est un sport nautique très populaire dans la Frise riche en lacs. L'événement annuel attirant principalement des Frisons, "la skûtsjesilen", fait venir un grand public, de Frisons, de Néerlandais et d'étrangers. Dans leurs bateaux, ils vont aux lacs de Frise pour voir de près le spectacle des galiotes.

Debido a los numerosos lagos que tiene Frisia se practica mucho el deporte de vela. El acontecimiento anual más espectacular, especialmente para los frisones aficionados al deporte acuático, son las carreras de "skûtsje" en las que participan cargueros de velas manejados por barqueros profesionales. Muchos espectadores de Frisia, de Holanda y del extranjero vienen en sus barcos a las aguas de Frisia para poder contemplar el espectáculo desde cerca.

フリースランド地方には数多くの湖があるので、ヨット乗りがさかんです。この地方の水上スポーツ・ファンが毎年待ちこがれるのが「スクッチェセイレン」。プロの船乗りがフリースランドの伝統的な帆船を操つるこの競争には、大勢の観客が地元、オランダ全国そして外国から集まり、少しでも近くから眺められるように、フリシアン・レイクスに船で集まります。

Groningen, Capital of the province of Groningen

Apart from the capital, the city of Groningen is also the oldest city in the province.
Nowadays, it is characterised by trade, the Post Office, banking and insurance activities. The city of Groningen is linked via the Eems Canal to the harbour of Delfzijl and has a busy road and canal system.

Groningen is, behalve de hoofdstad, tevens de oudste stad van de gelijknamige provincie.
Tegenwoordig karakteriseren de handel, posterijen, het bank- en verzekeringswezen het stadsgebeuren. Groningen staat via het Eemskanaal in verbinding met de haven van Delfzijl. Het wegen- en kanalenpatroon maken de stad tot een druk verkeerscentrum.

Groningen ist nicht nur die Hauptstadt der gleichnamigen Provinz sondern auch deren älteste Stadt.
Derzeit kennzeichnen Handel, die niederländische Post PTT, Banken und Versicherungsgesellschaften das Geschehen. Groningen ist über den Eemskanal mit dem Hafen Delfzijl verbunden. Durch das umliegende Straßen- und Kanalnetz wird die Stadt zu einem geschäftigen Verkehrszentrum.

Groningue, la plus vieille ville et le chef-lieu de la province du même nom, se caractérise par son centre commercial, ses postes, ses banques et ses assurances.
La ville est reliée par l'Eemskanaal au port de Delfzijl. Grâce au réseau routier et aux canaux, la ville est devenue un grand centre de trafic.

Además de ser capital de provincia, Groninga también es la ciudad más antigua de la provincia de Groninga.
La vida cotidiana de la ciudad la caracterizan actualmente el comercio, el Correo, los bancos y las compañías de seguros. Groninga está comunicada con el puerto de Delfzijl por el canal Eems. La red de carreteras y canales hace de la ciudad un centro de tráfico intenso.

フローニガンは、同名の州の州都であるほか、この州の一番歴史の長い市でもあります。
今日この市の主要産業として貿易、全国郵便ネットワーク本拠地としての活動、銀行・保険業などが上げられます。フローニガン市をデルフザイル港と結ぶのがエームス運河。道路網と運河網が、この市を活発な交通網中心地点とならさせめています。

68

Fransum, Knoll village

Fransum is a typical example of a knoll village and is situated on an artificially constructed hill settlement. Knoll villages were built in such a way in saltings, areas which were often flooded by rivers or sea, particularly along the North Sea coast. The first knolls date back to the 6th century varying from 2 to 7 meters in height. They were no longer necessary after the 12th century when dyke building began.

Fransum is een typisch voorbeeld van een terpendorp en staat als zodanig op een kunstmatig opgeworpen woonheuvel. Terpendorpen werden zo gebouwd in kweldergebieden, die regelmatig door rivier- of zeewater werden overstroomd, voornamelijk langs de Noordzeekust. De eerste terpen dateren uit de 6e eeuw, in hoogte variërend van 2 tot 7 meter. Na de 12e eeuw werd, door dijkaanleg, dit soort bouw overbodig.

Fransum ist ein typisches Beispiel eines Wurtendorfs. Das heißt, daß es auf einem künstlich aufgeschütteten Erdhügel erbaut wurde. Im Deichvorland, das immer wieder von Fluß- oder Meereswasser überschwemmt wurde, baute man auf diese Weise Wurtendörfer, vor allem entlang der Nordseeküste. Die ersten Wurten oder aufgeschütteten Erdhügel stammen aus dem 6. Jahrhundert. Diese waren zwischen 2 und 7 Meter hoch. Nach dem 12. Jahrhundert erübrigten sich diese Aufschüttungen durch den Bau von Deichen.

Fransum, tertre caractéristique, est bâti sur une hauteur. Les tertres étaient élevés dans les prés-salés, des pâturages côtiers périodiquement inondés par la mer, le plus souvent par la mer du Nord. Les premiers variant de 2 à 7 mètres de haut datent du VIᵉ s. Après le XIIᵉ s., la construction des digues rendit l'élévation des tertres inutile.

Fransum es un ejemplo típico de un pueblo terpe y como tal está situado en una colina levantada artificialmente. Los pueblos terpe fueron construidos así en tierras situadas fuera de los diques, que eran inundadas regularmente por el agua del río o del mar, sobre todo a lo largo de la costa del Mar del Norte. Los primeros terpes datan del siglo VI, pudiendo variar su altura de 2 a 7 metros. Después del siglo XII ya no se necesitó este tipo de construcciones, debido a la construcción de diques.

フランサムは典型的な小丘の村で、人工的に盛り上げた小山の上に住居が建っています。主に北海の岸付近の沼地にあった村落は、定期的に川や海の洪水によって脅かされたので、このような小丘居住地が生まれたのです。史上最初の小丘村はすでに6世紀に遡ることができ、盛り上げられた丘は2メートルから7メートルの高さでした。12世紀以後は、堤防が建設されるようになったので、このような居住地の必要はなくなりました。

Delfzijl, Industrial area

This aerial photograph shows the industrial area of Delfzijl with, in the background, the city itself and the Eems Canal which flows to the city of Groningen.

The top right hand corner shows the salt dock with in the bottom right the methanol dock belonging to AKZO Chemical Industry Delfzijl. This concern actually controls this industrial area.

Deze luchtfoto toont het industrie-gebied van Delfzijl, met op de achtergrond de stad zelf en het Eemskanaal, dat naar de stad Groningen voert.

Rechts-boven op de foto ziet men de zoutsteiger en rechts-onderaan de methanolsteiger van de Chemische Industrie van AKZO Delfzijl, die feitelijk dit industrie-gebied beheerst.

Dieses Luftbild zeigt das Industriegebiet von Delfzijl. Im Hintergrund die Stadt und der Eemskanal, der nach Groningen fließt.

Rechts oben auf dem Bild erkennt man die Salz-Landungsbrücke und rechts unten die Methanol-Landungsbrücke der chemischen Industrie von AKZO Delfzijl, die dem Industriegebiet das Gepräge verleiht.

Cette photo nous montre la zone industrielle de Delfzijl, la ville de Delfzijl (en arrière-plan) et l'Eemskanaal, qui la relie à la ville de Groningue.

En haut à droite, l'appontement des sels et en bas à droite l'appontement de méthanol de l'Industrie Chimique AKZO Delfzijl dominant la Z.I.

Esta fotografía aérea muestra la zona industrial de Delfzijl, con la ciudad misma al fondo y el canal Eems, que lleva a la ciudad de Groninga.

En la parte superior derecha de la fotografía se puede ver el atracadero para la sal y en la parte inferior derecha el atracadero para el metanol de la indstria química AKZO Delfzijl, que de hecho domina la zona industrial.

この航空写真は、市の中心地とフローニガン市に接続するエームス運河をバックにした、デルフザイルの工業地です。

右上にみえるのが、デルフザイルの化学工業企業アクゾ・デルフザイルの製塩用の塔で、右下がメタノ用です。アクゾはこの工業地で、最も重要な地位を占めています。

Bourtange, Fortress

Bourtange marsh was once high moorland on the border of the province of Groningen and Germany where, for military reasons, reclamation and development were not permitted.
   The Bourtange fortress is situated in an area of forts and bulwarks and has been splendidly restored to ensure appreciation for generations to come.

Het Bourtanger Moeras was eens een hoogveenmoeras op de grens van de provincie Groningen en Duitsland, waar, om militaire reden, geen ontginning mocht plaatsvinden.
   De vesting Bourtange ligt in het land van forten en schansen en is prachtig gerestaureerd, opdat wij en de komende generaties er nog lang van zullen kunnen genieten.

Der "Bourtanger Sumpf" war einstmals ein Hochmoorgebiet auf der Grenze zwischen der Provinz Groningen und Deutschland, das aus Militärgründen nicht urbar gemacht werden durfte.
   Die Festung Bourtange liegt im Land von Forts und Schanzen und wurde prächtig restauriert, damit wir und künftige Generationen uns noch lange an seinem Anblick erfreuen können.

Le Bourtanger Moeras (Marais de Bourtange) était à l'origine un marais de tourbière à la frontière de la Groningue et l'Allemagne, qui, pour des considérations militaires, ne pouvait pas être défriché.
   La forteresse de Bourtange, située dans la région des forts et des fortifications, est magnifiquement restaurée pour que nous et les générations suivantes puissions en jouir.

Antiguamente, Bourtanger Moeras era una región pantanosa de turberas en la frontera entre la provincia de Groninga y Alemania, que, por razones militares, no podía ser roturada.
   La fortaleza de Bourtange se encuentra en una región de fortificaciones y ha sido restaurada espléndidamente, para que nosotros y las generaciones venideras puedan disfrutar de ella por mucho tiempo.

　ブータンハー低湿地は、フローニガン州とドイツ国境の間にある泥炭沼地で軍事的な理由によって、開発が許可されない地帯となっています。
　砦やざんごうが散在している地域にあるブータンハ要塞地は、完璧に修復されました。この見事に昔の姿を取り戻した遺跡は、私達と次世代の目を楽しませてくれるでしょう。

North-Ruinen, Heather and fens

To the north of Ruinen in the province of Drenthe we find truly glorious countryside.

One of the few remaining heaths with fens - lakes resulting from peat-digging. Not to mention a fair stretch of forest. Typical Drenthe landscape which warrants our utmost care.

Ten Noorden van Ruinen in de provincie Drenthe ligt een schitterend mooi natuurgebied.

Een bijna zeldzaam geworden stuk heidegrond met vennen. Plassen, ontstaan door het veenafgraven. Ook een flinke strook bos ontbreekt niet. Een typisch stukje Drenthse natuur, waar we zuinig op moeten zijn.

Im Norden von Ruinen, in der Provinz Drenthe, liegt ein herrliches Naturschutzgebiet.

Ein fast zur Rarität gewordenes Stück Heidelandschaft mit Seen, welch letztere durch die Torfgewinnung entstanden. An einem Waldstreifen fehlt es hier ebensowenig. Eine für Drenthe typische Naturlandschaft, mit der wir sehr behutsam umgehen sollten.

Au nord de Ruinen dans la province de Drenthe se trouve une région naturelle merveilleuse.

Une terre de bruyère avec quelques mares résultant de l'extraction de la tourbe, une large forêt. Bref, une région naturelle caractéristique de la Drenthe, qui doit être ménagée.

Al norte de Ruinen, en la provincia de Drente, se encuentra un área natural de impresionante belleza.

Una zona casi excepcional de brezales con pantanos, lagos nacidos por la extracción de turba; tampoco falta una buena franja de bosques. Es un trozo típico de la naturaleza de Drente, que tenemos que cuidar mucho.

ドレンテ州ラウネンの北部に、美しい自然保護地があります。

ここには、余り見かけることのできなくなったヒースや泥炭があり、昔泥炭の採掘によってできた池があります。また森林も豊富で、これらのコンビネーションが、私達が大切に保護すべき、ドレンテ地方独特の自然の景色を織りなしています。

Assen, Capital of the province of Drenthe

In around 1200 a convent stood here known as Maria in Campis. Since then, Assen grew steadily and in 1807 became an independent municipality and received a charter in 1809. In Assen, known internationally for its annual Tourist Trophy motor races, the head offices of the Nederlandse Aardolie Maatschappij, NAM, have been situated since 1967.

Omstreeks het jaar 1200 bevond zich op deze plaats een nonnenklooster, genaamd Maria in Campis. Nadien heeft Assen zich gestadig ontwikkeld en werd in 1807 een zelfstandige gemeente, die in 1809 stadsrechten verkreeg. In Assen, internationaal bekend vanwege de jaarlijkse T.T. (Tourist Trophy) motorraces, zetelt tevens sinds 1967 het hoofdkantoor van de Nederlandse Aardolie Maatschappij (N.A.M.).

Um das Jahr 1200 befand sich an dieser Stelle das Nonnenkloster "Maria in Campis". Seither entwickelte Assen sich ständig weiter und wurde im Jahre 1807 zu einer selbständigen Gemeinde, der 1809 die Stadtrechte verliehen wurden. Wegen der Tourist-Trophy-Rennen, die alljährlich ausgetragen werden, ist Assen international bekannt. Ferner befindet sich hier seit 1967 das Hauptquartier der "N.A.M.", der niederländischen Erdölgesellschaft.

Vers 1200, à cet endroit s'élevait le couvent de religieuses Maria in Campis. Assen s'est développé au cours des siècles suivants, devint une commune autonome en 1807 et obtint ses privilèges communaux en 1809. Réputé pour ses courses motocyclistes, T.T., Assen abrite également, depuis 1967, le siège principal du N.A.M. (Société de Pétrole Néerlandaise).

Alrededor del año 1200 se encontraba en este lugar un convento de monjas, llamado María in Campis. Desde entonces, Assen se ha desarrollado continuamente y en 1807 se convirtió en un municipio independiente, que obtuvo derechos municipales en 1809. Assen, mundialmente famosa por el acontecimiento anual de las carreras de moto T.T. (Tourist Trophy), es también, desde 1967, la sede de la compañía petrolera holandesa, la N.A.M.

　1200年頃この場所には、マリア・イン・カンピスという尼僧院がありました。その後アッセンは順調に発展をとげ、1807年には独立した町となり、1809年には市としての自治権を獲得しました。アッセンは毎年行われるT.T.（ツーリスト・トロフィー）モーター・レースで国際的に有名であり、また1967年以来オランダ石油公団（N.A.M.）の総括本部がここにあります。

Megalithic tombs near Buinen

Megalithic tombs were built in western Europe more than 3 thousand years BC. These prehistoric tombs constructed with enormous granite boulders, swept south during the ice age, were built in varying shapes. The photograph shows portal tombs ranging in height from 3.5-20 metres and 1-2.5 meters in width.

Reeds 3000 jaar v. Chr. werden er in West-Europa Hunebedden gebouwd. Deze pre-historische grafmonumenten, opgebouwd uit grote granieten zwerfkeien, die in de oertijd via het landijs hun bestemming bereikten, komen in verschillende soorten voor. De Hunebedden op de luchtfoto zijn portaalgraven, in lengte variërend van 3,5-20 meter en in breedte van 1-2,5 meter.

Bereits 3000 Jahre vor der Zeitwende wurden in Westeuropa Megalithgräber errichtet. Diese aus großen Findlingen bestehenden prähistorischen Grabanlagen gibt es in verschiedenen Typen. Bei den auf diesem Luftbild gezeigten Megalithgräbern handelt es sich um Vorhofgräber mit einer Länge von dreieinhalb bis wanzig Metern und einer Breite von einem bis zweieinhalb Metern.

Dès 3000 av. J. Chr. il existait déjà, en Europe occidentale, des dresseurs de mégalithes. Ces monuments funéraires préhistoriques de blocs erratiques en granit de grandes dimensions apportés par l'inlandsis se présentent sous des formes diverses. Les mégalithes de la photo sont des "tombeaux à porche", de 3,5 à 20 m. de long sur 1 à 2,5 m. de large.

3000 años a.C. ya se construyeron dólmenes en la Europa Occidental. Estos monumentos funerarios prehistóricos, edificados con grandes piedras errantes de granito que en la prehistoria llegaron a su destino a través del manto de hielo, se dan en diferentes versiones. Los dólmenes de la fotografía son tumbas de galería cuya total longitud puede variar de 3,5 - 20 metros y su anchura de 1 - 2,5 metros.

紀元前3000年頃、西ヨーロッパでは大墓が作られました。これらの原始遺跡は、大昔氷河が運んで最終地に辿り着いた、巨大な花こう石の漂移石を積んで作られ、色々な種類があります。この航空写真の大墓は、門型の墓で、長さは3.5メートルから20メートルで、幅は1メートルから2.5メートルに及びます。

Zwolle, Capital of the province of Overijssel

Zwolle, on the river IJssel, began conducting a flourishing trade centuries ago and from the 13th to the 17th century was included in the Hanseatic League, a union of north and west European trading centres.

There is a cattle market every Friday and once a month a horse market. Parts of the mediaeval city wall are still standing, such as the Sassenpoort on the right of the photograph.

Zwolle, gelegen aan de rivier de IJssel, dreef al eeuwen geleden een bloeiende handel. De stad maakte van de 13e tot de 17e eeuw deel uit van de "Hanze", een bond van Noord- en West-Europese handelssteden.

Iedere Vrijdag wordt een veemarkt gehouden en eens per maand een paardenmarkt. In Zwolle staan nog delen van de middeleeuwse stadsmuur, zoals de Sassenpoort, rechts op de foto.

Zwolle, die Stadt am Ufer der IJssel, treibt schon seit Jahrhunderten einen blühenden Handel. Vom 13. bis zum 17. Jahrhundert war sie Teil der Hanse, einer Handelsgemeinschaft nord- und westeuropäischer Städte.

Jeden Freitag findet ein Viehmarkt und einmal monatlich ein Pferdemarkt statt. Zwolle hat noch Überreste der mittelalterlichen Stadtmauer aufzuweisen, wie die Sassenpoort, rechts auf dem Bild.

Situé au bord de l'IJsel, Zwolle connaissait, il y a plusieurs siècles déjà, un essor commercial. La ville adhéra, du XIIIe s. au XVIIe s., à la Ligue hanséatique, association de marchands et de villes de l'Europe septentrionale et occidentale.

Tous les vendredis un marché aux bestiaux et une fois par mois un marché aux chevaux s'y teinnent. Quelques parties des murailles de la ville de Zwolle subsistent encore, telle que la "Sassenpoort", à droite sur la photo.

Zwolle, situada a la orilla del río IJssel, tenía ya hace siglos un comercio floreciente. Desde el siglo XIII hasta el XVII la ciudad formó parte de la llamada 'Liga de Hansa', una liga de ciudades comerciales de la Europa del Norte y del Oeste.

Todos los viernes tiene lugar un mercado de ganado y una vez al mes un mercado de caballos. En Zwolle quedan restos de la muralla medieval, como la puerta Sassen, que se ve a la derecha en la fotografía.

ズウォレはアイセル川沿いにあり、すでに数世紀前から商業で栄えています。この都市は、13世紀から17世紀にかけて、北ヨーロッパと西ヨーロッパの貿易都市の連合であったハンザ連盟の加盟都市でした。

毎金曜日、畜牛市場が開かれ、一ケ月に一度は馬市場があります。ズウォレには今日でも、この写真の右端に見えるサッセン門のような、中世紀からの市壁の一部分が残っています。

Giethoorn, 'Dutch Venice'

Most of the lakes in Giethoorn resulted from peat-digging. The village of Giethoorn is unique in its watery setting and a great tourist attraction. Sailing through the village, also known as 'Dutch Venice' is an experience not to be missed.

Also worthy of admiration is the 'Otterskooi', one of Europe's largest duck traps.

De meeste plassen in Giethoorn zijn ontstaan door veenafgraving (verveningen). Als waterstreekdorp is Giethoorn uniek in Nederland en een grote toeristische attractie. Het is een ware belevenis om op een mooie zonnige dag door het dorp - ook wel het "Hollands Venetië" genoemd - te varen.

Men kan dan ook de "Otterskooi", één van de grootste eendenkooien van Europa, bewonderen.

Die meisten Tümpel in Giethoorn entstanden infolge der Torfgewinnung. Als Wasserdorf ist Giethoorn einzigartig in den Niederlanden und eine große touristische Attraktion. Es ist schon ein besonderes Erlebnis, an einem sonnigen Tag per Boot durch das Venedig Hollands zu fahren.

Man kann dann außerdem noch den 'Otterskooi', den größten Entenfang Europas, bewundern.

La plupart des étangs de Giethoorn se sont formés à la suite de l'extraction de tourbe. Village d'une région aquatique, Giethoorn constitue une attraction touristique unique. Une promenade en bateau par une belle journée ensoleillée sur les canaux de la "Venise hollandaise" peut être une expérience inoubliable.

L' "Otterskooi", une des plus grandes canardières de toute l'Europe, offre des choses intéressantes.

La mayoría de los lagos de Giethoorn tienen su origen en la extracción de turberas. Como pueblo situado en una región puramente acuática, Giethoorn es único en Holanda y una gran atracción turística. Es una verdadera experiencia pasar por el pueblo - que también se conoce por el nombre de la Venecia holandesa, en un día de sol.

En esa ocasión también se puede contemplar la "Otterskooi", uno de los mayores puestos para la caza de ánades de Europa.

　ヒットホーンの池や湖のほとんどは、泥炭採掘の結果によってできました。水の村としてヒットホーンは、オランダでもユニークでポピュラーな観光地です。オランダのベニスといわれているこの村を、太陽の輝く日に船で巡るのは、忘れられない体験となる筈です。

　「オッタースコイ」と呼ばれている、ヨーロッパ一大きいかも猟のおとりを見物するのも楽しいでしょう。

Plough at work near Kampen

This attractive photograph taken near Kampen gives the impression of a gigantic, sunken chair. The various crops will be grown in neat plots.

Almost an abstract painting, but the farmer on his tractor undoubtedly will transform the 'chair' into an ordinary field.

Dit fraaie beeld, gemaakt in de omgeving van Kampen, geeft de indruk van een enorm grote zitkuil. De verschillende gewassen, die hier verbouwd worden, liggen in keurige percelen.

Het geheel geeft de impressie van een abstract schilderij, doch ongetwijfeld gaat de boer verder op zijn tractor en zal de "zitkuil" veranderen in een gewoon veld.

Dieses schöne Bild, das in der Umgebung von Kampen entstand, erinnert irgendwie an eine riesige Sitzgrube. Die diversen, hier angebauten Gewächse stehen sauber in Parzellen.

Das Ganze sieht wie ein modernes Gemälde aus. Zweifellos aber wird der Bauer seine Arbeit mit dem Traktor fortsetzen und wird aus der "Sitzgrube" ein normales Feld entstehen.

Cette image charmante d'un endroit aux environs de Kampen évoque l'idée d'une fosse salon. Les plantes diverses sont bien arrangées dans des parcelles de même culture.

L'ensemble semble être une peinture abstraite. Mais, sans aucun doute, l'agriculteur poursuivra son chemin sur le tracteur et la "fosse salon" se transformera en un champ comme tous les autres.

Esta hermosa imagen, hecha en los alrededores de Kampen, da la impresión de un cuarto de estar de unas dimensiones enormes. Los diferentes cultivos están ordenados en lotes impecables.

En su totalidad da la impresión de un cuadro abstracto, pero sin duda el campesino seguirá adelante en su tractor y 'el cuarto de estar' será convertido en un campo normal.

カンペン付近で撮影したこの美しい写真は、大きな絨 のようです。この地域で栽培される多数の品種の野菜は、規則正しく区切られています。

全体を眺めると抽象画のようですが、一旦百姓のトラクターが通過すれば、この絵画はただの畑に変化してしまうことでしょう。

Zutphen, Town centre

Zutphen, situaded at the merging point of the rivers Berkel and IJssel is one of those river towns with an extra special charm, known for centuries as 'the Town of Towers'. Aside from the many churches and towered buildings Zutphen has one the Netherlands' most-interesting town centres.

The St. Walburgs Church dating from the 13th-15th century, is a monumental building.

Zutphen, gelegen aan de samenvloeiing van de Berkel en de IJssel, is één van die riviersteden met een speciale charme, daar het vanouds de bijnaam heeft van het "torenrijke Zutphen". Behalve veel kerken en gebouwen met torens heeft Zutphen ook één van de meest bezienswaardige stadskernen van Nederland.

Een monumentaal bouwwerk is de St. Walburgskerk uit de 13-15 eeuw.

Zutphen liegt an der Mündung von Berkel und IJssel und ist eine jener Flußstädte mit dem gewissen Etwas. Denn seit jeher hat es den Beinamen "turmreiches Zutphen". Außer einer Vielzahl von Kirchen und Bauten mit Türmen hat Zutphen eine der sehenswertesten Altstädte der Niederlande.

Ein Monumentalbau ist die St. Walburgskirche aus dem 13.-15. Jahrhundert.

Zutphen, situé au confluent de la Berkel et de l'IJsel, est une ville très charmante. Depuis des siècles elle est surnommée "Zutphen riche en tours". Elle ne possède pas seulement un grand nombre d'églises et d'anciens bâtiments flanqués de tours, ses vieux noyaux urbains, qui comptent parmi les plus beaux des Pays-Bas, valent certainement une visite.

La "St. Walburgkerk", datant de XIIIe-XVe s., est d'un grand intérêt architectural.

Zutphen, situada en la confluencia de los ríos Berkel y IJssel, es una de esas ciudades fluviales que tienen un encanto especial; desde siempre lleva el sobrenombre de 'Zutphen la de las muchas torres'. Aparte de las nomerosas iglesias y edificios con torres, Zutphen tiene también uno de los centros urbanos más interesantes de Holanda.

Un edificio monumental es la iglesia del St⁰ Walburg del siglo XIII-XV.

ズットフェンは、ベルケル川とアイセル川が交わる点にあり、昔から「塔の町」というニックネームを持つ、特別な魅力をたたえた川沿いの都市です。塔のある数多くの教会や建物があるというだけでなく、この都市の中心街はオランダでも由緒あるものです。最も目を奪う建築物は、13世紀から15世紀にかけてできた聖ワルブルグ教会です。

Dalfsen, Rechteren Castle

Rechteren Castle was referred to as early as the 13th century as a 'pirate castle'. After rebuilding took place in 1320, everything except its outbuildings were demolished. In the following three centuries many alterations took place. Surrounded by a moat, it now comprises one main building - an 18th century palace - with two wings and a round look-out tower.

Reeds in de 13e eeuw werd kasteel Rechteren vermeld als roofslot. Na in 1320 te zijn herbouwd werd het - op de bijgebouwen na - afgebroken. In de drie daarop volgende eeuwen hebben veel veranderingen en uitbreidingen plaatsgevonden. Door een gracht omgeven, bestaat het geheel nu uit een hoofdgebouw - een paleisje uit de 18e eeuw - met twee vleugels en een ronde verdedigingstoren.

Bereits im 13. Jahrhundert wird Schloß Rechteren als Räuberschloß erwähnt. Nachdem es im Jahre 1320 wiederaufgebaut worden war - die Nebengebäude ausgenommen -, wurde es abgerissen. In den drei nachfolgenden Jahrhunderten wurden viele Änderungen und Erweiterungen vorgenommen. Das Ganze ist mit einem Graben umgeben und besteht heute aus dem Hauptgebäude - einem Schlößchen aus dem 18. Jahrhundert - mit zwei Flügeln und einem runden Verteidigungsturm.

Dès le XIIIᵉ s. le château de Rechteren est mentionné comme un "château pirate". Reconstruit en 1320, il finit par être démoli. Seuls les bâtiments annexes restèrent intacts. Pendant les trois siècles suivants, il a subi beaucoup de changements et d'extensions. Entouré d'un fossé, l'ensemble se compose, de nos jours, du bâtiment principal - un petit palais du XVIIIᵉ s. - ses deux ailes et une tour de défense ronde.

Ya en el siglo XIII se hacía mención del castillo de Rechteren como castillo de un caballero bandido. Después de haber sido reconstruido en 1320, fue derribado - con excepción de las dependencias. En los tres siglos siguientes tuvieron lugar muchos cambios y ampliaciones. El conjunto consta actualmente de un edificio principal - un pequeño palacio del siglo XVIII - con dos alas y una torre de defensa redonda y está rodeado por un foso.

　13世紀の記録によると、レフテレン城は、暴れ者貴族の持ち城となっています。1320年の修復以後、この城は別館をのぞいて一旦打ち壊され、三世紀にわたってさまざまな形の建築や拡張がなされました。今日レフテレン城は、二つの翼建築と要塞塔を持つ18世紀の宮殿が、堀に囲まれた形として定着しています。

Enschede, Overall view

When King William I decided to develop the cotton industry in the Netherlands he enlisted the help of Thomas Ainsworth, an English industrialist. The British mechanised weaving technique was taught at the weaving school in Goor and a flourishing textile industry resulted.

During the 1950's developments such as the rise of the chemical industry changed things radically. The Twente College of Technology, which opened its doors in 1964, is now a famous institution.

Toen Koning Willem I besloot de katoennijverheid in Nederland tot ontwikkeling te brengen, deed hij dat met de hulp van Thomas Ainsworth, een Engels industrieel. Op de weefschool in Goor werd de Engelse machinale weeftechniek geleerd en er kwam een bloeiende textielindustrie tot stand.

In de jaren vijftig werd door o.a. de vestiging van de chemische industrie het patroon totaal veranderd. Faam verwierf zich de Technische Hogeschool Twente, die in 1964 haar deuren opende.

Als König Wilhelm I. beschloß, die Baumwollindustrie in den Niederlanden zu entwickeln, holte er sich die Hilfe von Thomas Ainsworth - einem englischen Industriellen - ein. In der Webschule in Goor wurden die Leute an einem englischen Maschinenwebstuhl ausgebildet, und es entwickelte sich eine blühende Textilindustrie.

In den 50er Jahren änderte sich das industrielle Bild vollkommen, u.a. weil die chemische Industrie sich hier niederließ. Berühmt ist die Technische Hochschule Twente, die 1964 ihre Tore öffnete.

Quand le roi Guillaume Ier décida de développer l'industrie cotonnière des Pays-Bas, il eut recours à Thomas Ainsworth, un industriel anglais. A l'école de tissage de Goor, on enseignait l'art de tisser à l'anglaise et l'industrie textile connut un essor.

Dans les années 50, l'industrie chimique provoqua un changement profond dans l'infrastructure régionale. L'Ecole supérieure technique ouvrit ses portes en 1964 et connut une réputation immédiate.

Cuando el Rey Guillermo I decidió desarrollar la industria algodonera en Holanda, lo hizo con ayuda de Thomas Ainsworth, un industrial británico. La técnica inglesa del telar mecánico fue enseñada en la escuela de artes textiles de Goor, y surgió una industria textil floreciente.

En los años cincuenta cambió la situación por completo, debido, entre otras cosas, al establecimiento de la industria química. La Universidad Técnica de Twente, que abrió sus puertas en 1964, adquirió buena reputación.

ヴィルム一世は、王としてオランダに木綿産業を振興させようと決めた際、イギリスの実業家トーマス・アインスワースの協力を求めました。ホーアの織物学校に英国式の繊維機械技術が教えられるようになると、この地域では繊維産業が非常に栄えるようになりました。

1950年代に化学産業が導入されると、この新しい工業が、繊維産業の重要地域産業としての地位を奪いました。有名なトゥエンテ工業大学は、1964年に設立されました。

92

Lemelerberg, The shepherd and his flock

A touching photograph which speaks for itself. A shepherd and his dog trying to keep together a flock of 206 sheep on the Lemelerberg heath in the province of Overijssel.
Unfortunately, the heaths are gradually being eliminated by other vegetation.

Woorden schieten te kort om dit lieflijke en zeldzame tafereel weer te geven. De foto spreekt voor zich. Op de Lemelerbergse heide in de provincie Overijssel probeert een schaapherder met zijn hond deze 206 schapen bij elkaar te houden.
Helaas worden onze heidegronden langzamerhand verdrongen door andere plantengroei.

Worte reichen nicht aus, um diese selten gewordene Szene voller Liebreiz zu beschreiben. Wir lassen das Bild daher für sich sprechen. Auf der Lemelerberger Heide in der Provinz Overijssel hält ein Hirte mit seinem Hund die 206 Schafe zusammen.
Leider wird unsere Heidefläche zusehends von anderen Gewächsen zurückgedrängt.

Cette scène si charmante, qu'on ne voit que rarement, se passe de commentaire. Sur les bruyères de Lemelerberg dans la province de l'Overijssel, un berger et son chien gardent les 206 moutons.
Malheureusement, nos terres de bruyère sont de plus en plus remplacées par d'autres végétations.

No se encuentran palabras para describir esta escena apacible y poco común. Dejemos que la foto hable por sí misma. En el así llamado brezal de Lemelerberg, en la provincia de Overijssel, un pastor y su perro procuran mantener unidas estas 206 ovejas.
Por desgracia, poco a poco los brezales están siendo desbancados por otra vegetación.

このチャーミングでめずらしいシーンを、言葉で表すことは不可能に近いですが、写真がすべてを表現してくれます。オーバーアイセル州のレメレーベルフセのヒース原で、羊飼いは犬と共に、206頭の羊をまとめようとしているところです。
残念ながらオランダのヒース原は、徐々に他の植物にとって代わられています。

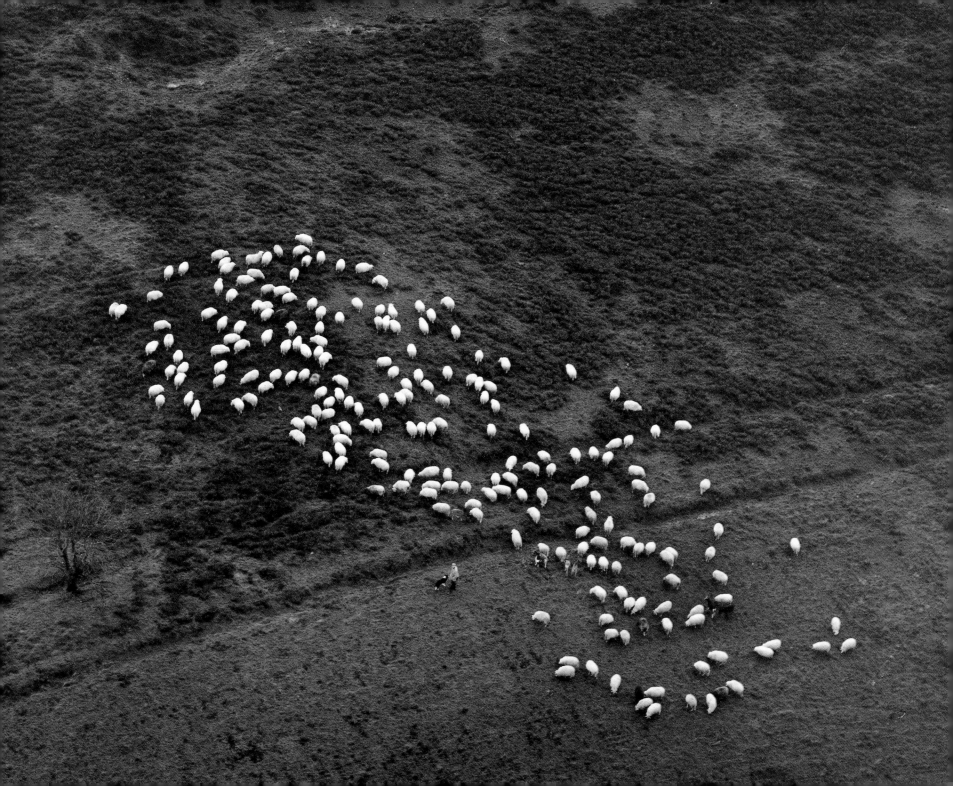

Deventer, The town and its river

This aerial photograph clearly shows that Deventer is one of the country's most beautiful cities. An old Hansa town on the river IJssel, its centre is adorned with splendid buildings.

The bridge at Deventer was used in the filming of 'A Bridge too Far' as Arnhem had undergone too many changes.

Hetgeen duidelijk uitkomt op deze luchtfoto is dat Deventer één van de mooiste steden van het land genoemd mag worden. Als oude Hanzestad aan de IJssel, is de binnenstad getooid met prachtige gebouwen.

Voor de verfilming van "A Bridge too Far" heeft de brug van Deventer model gestaan, aangezien er in Arnhem zelf te veel veranderingen hadden plaatsgevonden.

Deventer darf mit Recht eine der schönsten Städte des Landes genannt werden; das geht aus diesem Luftbild klar hervor. In der Innenstadt der altehrwürdigen Hansestadt an der IJssel stehen schmucke Gebäude.

Für den Film "A Bridge too Far" hat die Brücke von Deventer Modell gestanden, da sich in Arnhem, dem eigentlichen historischen Schauplatz, zuviel verändert hatte.

La photo nous montre nettement que Deventer pourrait être nommée une des plus belles villes du pays. Ancienne ville hanséatique au bord de l'IJssel, son centre recèle des bâtiments magnifiques.

Le pont de Deventer figure dans le film "A Bridge too Far", servant de modèle pour celui d'Arnhem, ville qui, depuis la guerre, a subi trop de changements.

Lo que destaca claramente en esta fotografía aérea es que Deventer puede ser calificada como una de las ciudades más bonitas del país. En su centro se encuentran unos edificios magníficos, por haber estado aliada a la Liga Hanseática esta antigua ciudad a orillas del IJssel.

Para el rodaje de la película "A Bridge too Far" se ha tomado como modelo el puente de Deventer, ya que la ciudad de Arnhem había sufrido demasiadas modificaciones.

この航空写真が明確に表しているのは、オランダでも最も美しい都市の一つと言われているデベンターです。アイセル川に面した昔のハンザ加盟都市として、この市の中心街には、すばらしい由緒ある建物が並んでいます。

アーネムには余り以前のおもむきが残っていないので、映画「A Bridge Too Far」の撮影には、デベンターの橋がモデルとして使われました。

Lelystad, Capital of the province of Flevoland

A considerable part of the Netherlands was once the bed of the former Zuiderzee. Lelystad is a grand example of a new town in the East Flevoland polder which welcomed its first inhabitants in 1967. There are four residential and two industrial areas. Separate road systems for different types of traffic render the town as safe as possible. The name Lelystad was derived from Cornelus Lely, a civil engineer and statesman, who died in 1929.

Een belangrijk deel van Nederland is ontstaan op de bodem van de voormalige Zuiderzee. Lelystad is een prachtig voorbeeld van een nieuwe stad in de polder Oostelijk Flevoland, waar de eerste bewoners zich in 1967 vestigden. Er zijn vier woongebieden met veel ééngezinswoningen en twee industrieterreinen. Een volledige scheiding van verkeerssoorten heeft tot doel de stad zo veilig mogelijk te maken. Lelystad dankt zijn naam aan de in 1929 overleden Cornelus Lely, civiel-ingenieur en staatsman.

Große Teile der Niederlande entstanden auf dem Boden der ehemaligen Zuidersee. Lelystad ist das Paradebeispiel einer neuen Stadt im Polder "Oostelijk Flevoland". 1967 ließen sich die ersten Bewohner nieder. Es gibt vier Ortsteile mit vielen Einfamilienhäusern und zwei Industriegebiete. Mit einer vollständigen Trennung der einzelnen Verkehrstypen wird bezweckt, die Stadt möglichst sicher zu machen. Lelystad verdankt seinen Namen dem 1929 gestorbenen Bauingenieur und Staatsmann Cornelus Lely.

Une partie considérable des Pays-Bas est née sur le fond de l'ancien Zuiderzee. Lelystad, bel exemple des nouvelles villes dans le polder Oostelijk Flevoland, a reçu ses premiers habitants en 1967 et compte quatre zones d'habitation et deux zones industrielles. La sécurité routière dans la ville est assurée par une séparation très nette des moyens de transport. Lelystad emprunte son nom à l'ingénieur civil et homme d'état Cornelus Lely mort en 1929.

Una parte importante de Holanda se formó sobre el fondo de un mar desecado, el llamado Zuiderzee. Lelystad es un buen ejemplo de una ciudad nueva en el pólder Oostelijk Flevoland, donde los primeros habitantes se establecieron en 1967. Hay cuatro zonas residenciales con muchas viviendas unifamiliares y dos zonas industriales. La completa separación de los diferentes tipos de tráfico tiene por objeto garantizar una seguridad óptima. Lelystad debe su nombre a Cornelis Lely, ingeniero civil y hombre de estado que murió en 1929.

オランダの重要な一部は、もとザウダー海の海底から成っています。レリースタッドは、東フレーボランド干拓地の新世界としての良い例で、1967年に最初の住民がこの市にやってきました。この都市は、多くの家族用住宅のある四地域と二工業地に分かれています。
　ここでは、鉄道・車・自転車・歩道といった交通方法が完全に分離していて、人々の安全を守っています。レリースタッドという名の由来は、この干拓地の生みの親であった、土木技師・政治家コルネラス・レリー（1929年没）によるものです。

Urk, Once an island

The island of Urk was joined at the south-west point of the North East polder in 1942. A large part of its population still works in the fishing industry. Urk fishermen fish in the North Sea and in the IJssel lake. The ancient village centre boasts small, fishermens' cottages with green-painted upper gables. Traditional dress is a common sight in Urk.

Het eiland Urk werd in 1942 ten Zuidwesten aangesloten aan de Noordoostpolder. Een groot deel van de bevolking werkt nog in de visserij en in aanverwante bedrijven en nijverheid. Urk beschikt over een Noordzee- en IJsselmeervloot. De eeuwenoude dorpskern bestaat uit vissershuisjes, waarvan de topgevels groen geschilderd zijn. Ook de traditionele klederdracht wordt in Urk nog veel gedragen.

Die einstige Insel Urk wurde 1942 im Südwesten mit dem Noordoostpolder verbunden. Dennoch arbeitet ein Großteil der Bevölkerung weiterhin in der Fischerei und zugehörigen Industriezweigen. Urk verfügt über eine Nordsee- und IJsselmeer-Flotte. Der jahrhundertealte Dorfkern besteht aus lauter Fischerhäusern mit grünen Dachgiebeln. Die traditionelle Tracht wird in Urk noch von vielen Einwohnern getragen.

En 1942, l'île d'Urk fut rattachée, du côté sud-ouest, au Noordoostpolder. Une grande partie de la population s'occupe de la pêche, d'entreprises connexes et d'industrie artisanale. Urk possède deux flottes, l'une pour la mer du Nord, l'autre pour le Lac d'IJssel. Son vieux centre se compose de maisons de pêcheurs, dont les pignons sont peints en vert. Même les costumes traditionnels sont encore portés.

En 1942, la que fue isla de Urk fue conectada a la parte suroeste del pólder Noordoost. Gran parte de la población sigue trabajando en la pesca y en empresas e industrias derivadas. Urk dispone de una flota para el Mar del Norte y de otra para el lago IJssel. El secular núcleo del pueblo consta de casas de pescadores cuyas fachadas están pintadas de verde. En Urk aún se viste mucho el traje típico tradicional.

　ウルク島の西南が1942年に東北干拓地に接続して以来、ウルクは島ではなくなりました。しかし現在でもウルクの住民は、漁業か関連産業・企業に携わっています。ウルクの船隊は、北海とアイセル湖で漁業に従事します。この非常に古い町の中心地には、緑色の切妻がある漁師の家が立ち並んでおり、今でも伝統的な民族衣裳を身につけている人達が大勢います。

Lelystad, The 'Houtrib Locks'

The Houtrib Locks in Lelystad form a junction of the busiest inland navigation routes in the Netherlands.
　The photograph also shows the PTT radio and television transmitter mast which feeds Lelystad.

De Houtribsluizen in Lelystad vormen een knooppunt voor de drukst bevaren binnenscheepvaartroute in Nederland.
　De foto toont tevens de PTT Radio en TV zendmast, die alle programma's op het net van Lelystad verzorgt.

Die Houtrib-Sleusen in Lelystad sind ein Knotenpunkt für die meist befahrene Binnenschiffahrtsstraße der Niederlande.
　Das Bild zeigt ferner den Hörfunk- und Fernseh-Sendemast der PTT für das Kabelnetz von Lelystad.

Les ''écluses de Houtrib'' (Houtribsluizen) constituent le noeud des routes de la navigation fluviale les plus importantes du pays.
　Sur la photo également l'antenne d'émission de radio et de télévision des PTT, d'où sont diffusés tous les programmes de la chaîne de Lelystad.

Las esclusas llamadas de Houtrib, en Lelystad, constituyen un centro de tráfico en la ruta fluvial de más navegación de Holanda.
　La fotografía muestra también el mástil emisor de radio y televisión, por medio del que se realizan todos los programas de la cadena de Lelystad.

　レリースタッドのハウトリブスラウスは、オランダの内海航海でもっとも交通量の多い場所です。
　この写真にはPTT（オランダ郵便・通信）のラジオとテレビ・タワーがありますが、これがレリースタッド内のネットワークの全プログラムを扱っています。

(Overleaf) North-East Polder, Reclaimed land

In the vast landscape of the North East polder red-roofed farms are neatly dotted along the lanes. Nestling between the trees which provide shelter from the wind and rain.

This polder landschape, mysteriously beautiful yet so productive, appears from the air as a symmetrical entity.

In het uitgestrekte landschap van de Noordoostpolder staan de boerderijen met hun rode daken als het ware keurig gerangschikt langs de wegen. Opgesloten tussen de bomen, die beschutting moeten bieden tegen weer en wind.

Dit stuk polderlandschap, zo wonderlijk mooi en tegelijkertijd zo produktief, toont - zeker vanuit de lucht gezien - als een prachtig symmetrisch geheel.

In der ausgedehnten Landschaft des Noordoost-Polders stehen die Dauernhöfe mit ihren roten Dächern, als wären sie fein säuberlich entlang den Straßen angeordnet worden. In dieser flachen Landschaft bieten die Bäume den Höfen Schutz vor Wind und Wetter.

Dieses schöne und gleichzeitig so produktive Marschland zeigt sich - gerade aus der Vogelflugperspektive - in seinen herrlichen symmetrischen Formen.

Les fermes aux toits rouges dans le vaste paysage du Nordoostpolder impeccablement arrangées le long des chemins sont enfermées par les arbres qui les mettent à l'abri du vent et de la pluie.

Ce paysage de polders, une merveille de beauté et d'une grande productivité, se montre, sur cette photo aérienne, comme un bel ensemble symétrique.

En el espacioso paisaje del pólder Noordoost, las granjas con sus techos rojos están ordenadas impecablemente, por así decirlo, a lo largo de las carreteras, rodeadas por los árboles, que ofrecen abrigo contra el mal tiempo y el aire.

Este paisaje de pólder, tan extrañamente bonito y al mismo tiempo tan fértil, se muestra - al menos visto desde el aire - como un magnífico conjunto simétrico.

この風景では、道路にそって農家の赤い屋根が、規則正しく並んでいます。それぞれ木に囲まれていますが、木は防風になり、夏の日ざしからも家を守ってくれます。

限りなく美しく、実りの多いこの干拓地は、特に上空から見ると幾何学的な模様をなしています。

IJsselmeer, 'Breaking the ice'

Sometimes in the Netherlands the temperature falls so low that one can skate on the IJssel lake and even drive a car over the ice! Here, the ice breakers were called in to open the shipping lanes leaving large ice floes in their wake.

Often, by morning, the open channels will have frozen over again.

Soms komt het in Nederland voor, dat het zo hard vriest, dat zelfs het IJsselmeer geschikt is om erop te schaatsen, ja, zelfs auto te rijden. Deze keer moesten er ijsbrekers aan te pas komen om de vaarroutes open te breken, daarbij grote schotsen achter zich latend.

Vaak tevergeefs, omdat nog dezelfde nacht de vorst weer toeslaat en het geheel weer dichtvriest.

Manchmal friert es in den Niederlanden so stark, daß man auch auf dem IJsselmeer Schlittschuh laufen und sogar mit dem Auto darauf fahren kann. Diesmal mußten die Schiffahrtsstraßen mit Eisbrechern befahrbar gemacht werden, wobei große Schollen entstanden.

Oft vergeblich, da durch die Eiseskälte in derselben Nacht alles wieder zufriert.

Il gèle parfois si fort en Hollande que le Lac d'IJssel est couvert d'une couche épaisse de glace permettant le patinage et même la circulation des voitures. Ce jour-là il fallait se servir des brise-glace pour ouvrir la route aux bateaux, laissant derrière eux de grands glaçons.

Souvent, ces tentatives étaient vaines, la nuit apportant une nouvelle gelée et les eaux se prenant à nouveau.

A veces hiela tanto en Holanda que hasta el lago IJssel se presta al patinaje e incluso a una vuelta en coche. Esta vez tuvieron que intervenir barcos rompehielos para abrir las rutas de navegación, dejando atrás grandes témpanos.

Como otras veces fue en vano, porque esa misma noche volvió a caer una helada que lo cerró todo de nuevo.

時々オランダではすべてが凍りつき、アイセル湖の上では、スケートができるだけでなく、車を運転することすらできます。ここでは航路を切り拓くために、アイス・ブレカーが登場し、大きな浮氷を後に残していきました。

一晩たつと、再び凍り閉ざされてしまうこともよくあります。

106

Flevopolder, Rapeseed fields

The IJssel lake dam was completed in 1932 and after the war the Dutch began reclaiming large areas of the former Zuiderzee. The polders, low areas of the Netherlands, are unique in this world as this artistic photograph of rapeseed fields shows.
Summer rapeseed is planted as a fertiliser or is grown as green fodder.

Sinds in 1932 de Afsluitdijk gereed kwam is men, na de oorlog, begonnen met het inpolderen van grote delen van de voormalige Zuiderzee. Het polderland is - als het lage deel van Nederland - in zijn uitgestrektheid vrijwel uniek op deze wereld, getuige deze artistieke opname van koolzaadvelden.
Zomerkoolzaad wordt geplant ter grondbemesting of wordt als groenvoedergewas geteeld.

Seit Fertigstellung des Abschlußdeiches im Jahre 1932 begann man nach dem Kriege, große Teile der ehemaligen Zuidersee einzudeichen. Die Polderlandschaft ist als der tiefliegende Teil der Niederlande in seiner Ausdehnung in der ganzen Welt nahezu einzigartig, wie aus dieser künstlerischen Aufnahme von Rapsfeldern hervorgehen möge.
Raps wird zur Düngung des Bodens oder als Grünfuttergewächs angebaut.

Depuis l'achèvement de la digue du Nord en 1932, on s'est mis à transformer en polders de grandes surfaces de l'ancien Zuiderzee. Le pays des polders - la partie basse du pays - marqué par son immensité, est unique au monde; cette photo artistique de champs de colza en témoigne.
Les semences du colza d'été servent au fumage des terres ou de fourrage vert.

Desde que en 1932 se dio término al dique de cierre "Afsluitdijk", se empezó después de la guerra a desecar y a poner diques alrededor de grandes partes del que fuera mar de Zuiderzee. La tierra de los pólderes - siendo la parte baja de Holanda - es prácticamente única en el mundo por su espaciosidad, como testifica esta artística foto de unos campos de colza.
La colza se planta para abonar la tierra o se cultiva como planta forrajera.

　1932年に締切り堤防が完成し、その後戦争も終わってから、ザウダー海だった所の大部分を干拓することになりました。干拓地はオランダ内でも土地の低い部分に当りますが、この規模で干拓することは、世界でもユニークなことです。これは菜種畑の芸術写真です。夏菜種は、土壌の肥料として植えられるか、飼料として栽培されます。

Dronten, Polder town

It is hard to believe, but where in the 1950's fishing boats once sailed you will now find the town of Dronten. A bustling municipality with its familiar recreation centre 'De Meerpaal'.

The sizeable industrial estates attract new businesses with the added advantage of excellent housing facilities for employees.

Het is moeilijk te geloven, maar - waar in de jaren vijftig nog op ruime schaal werd gevist - is nu Dronten verrezen. Een bruisende gemeente, met als bekend middelpunt het uitgaanscentrum "De Meerpaal".

De ruime industrieterreinen maken het aantrekkelijk voor ondernemers zich hier te vestigen, vooral ook, omdat daaraan veelal huisvesting voor de werknemers verbonden is, in uitstekende woningen.

Kaum zu glauben! Doch dort, wo jetzt Dronten erblüth, wurde einstmals viel Fischfang betrieben. Bekannter Mittelpunkt dieses sprudelnden Orts ist das Ausgeh- und Bummelviertel "De Meerpaal".

Wegen seiner ausgedehnten Industriegebiete ist Dronten reizvoll für Unternehmer, um sich hier niederzulassen, vor allem auch wegen der damit oftmals verbundenen ausgezeichneten Wohnraumbeschaffung für die Arbeitnehmer.

Dans les anneés cinquante, la commune animée de Dronten, dont le complexe d'activités récréatives "De Meerpaal" est bien connu, n'existait pas encore. Fait incroyable, mais ici on ne voyait que des bateaux de pêche.

De nombreux entrepreneurs sont attirés par les grandes zones industrielles et y trouvent d'excellents logements pour leurs ouvriers.

Es difícil de creer, pero en el lugar donde en los años cincuenta aún se pescaba a gran escala, ha surgido ahora Dronten, un minicipio activo, con el conocido centro de salida "De Meerpaal".

Las espaciosas zonas de industria incitan a los empresarios a establecerse aquí, también porque ello va unido, generalmente, a excelentes viviendas para el personal.

この賑やかな町ドロンテンが、1950年代まで大規模な漁業場であったということは信じがたいことです。水から出現したドロンテンの現在の中心は、「デ・ミーアパール」。

この町には工業地も充分あり、企業者にとって魅力的な選択を提供しています。また働く者のための優れた住宅も整っています。

110

'Het Loo' Palace

Founded in 1686 by King-Stadholder William III Het Loo Palace has been used by various generations of the House of Orange as a hunting lodge. Because of its attractive gardens, laid out in the so-called 'Le Nôtre' style it is sometimes referred to as the Versailles of the North.

After Queen Wilhelmina died here in 1962 the beautifully restored palace, which now houses the Orange Museum, was reopened in June 1984 by her granddaughter Queen Beatrix.

Gesticht in 1686 door Koning-Stadhouder Willem III, werd paleis Het Loo door verschillende generaties Oranjes als jachtslot gebruikt. Door de fraai aangelegde tuinen in de z.g. "Le Nôtre"-stijl wordt het ook wel het Versailles van het Noorden genoemd.

Nadat Koningin Wilhelmina hier in 1962 overleed, werd het prachtig gerestaureerde paleis, dat thans het Oranjemuseum herbergt, in juni 1984 heropend door haar kleindochter, Koningin Beatrix.

Schloß Het Loo wurde im Jahre 1686 vom König-Statthalter Wilhelm III. gegründet, und viele Generationen von Oraniern benutzten es als Jagdschloß. Man nennt es wegen seiner prächtigen Gartenanlagen im sogenannten "Le-Nôtre"-Stil auch das Versailles des Nordens.

Nachdem hier im Jahre 1962 Königin Wilhelmina gestorben war, wurde das meisterhaft restaurierte Schloß, das heute dem Oranien-Museum Platz bietet, im Juni 1984 von ihrer Enkelin, Königin Beatrix, wiedereröffnet.

Fondé en 1686 par le roi et stathouder Guillaume III, le Palais Het Loo a servi de pavillon de chasse à plusieurs générations de la Maison d'Orange. En raison de ses beaux jardins aménagés dans le style de Le Nôtre, il est souvent appelé le Versailles du Nord.

Après la mort de la reine Wilhelmine en 1962, le palais, magnifiquement restauré et abritant aujourd'hui le Musée d'Orange, a été ouvert à nouveau, en juin 1984, par sa petite-fille, la reine Béatrice.

El palacio "Het Loo", fundado en 1686 por el Rey y Magistrado Supremo Guillermo III, sirvió de pabellón de caza a diferentes generaciones de la casa de Orange. Por sus magníficos jardines diseñados al estilo del famoso "Le Nôtre", el palacio también se conoce por el nombre del Versalles del norte.

En 1962 falleció aquí la reina Guillermina. En 1984 su nieta, la reina Beatriz, volvió a abrir el palacio espléndidamente restaurado, que hoy en día alberga el museo de Orange.

　オランダ総督であり英国王であったヴィレム三世が、1686年に建てたヘット・ロー城は、数世代間オランェ王家によって、狩館として使われてきました。「レ・ノットル」という様式の美しい庭園によって、この城は、北のベルサイユとも呼ばれるようになりました。

　ヴィラミナ女王がこの城で1962年に亡くなられた後、見事に修復されてオランェ博物館も含むようになったヘット・ロー城は、1984年６月にヴィラミナ女王の孫娘にあたられるベアトリックス女王によって再オープンしました。

Arnhem, Capital of the province of Gelderland

Arnhem arose from the Prüm Abbey dating from the year 893 which consisted of a church and a few possessions. It was the Rhine Bridge during the Battle of Arnhem in the Second World War which was 'a bridge too far' bringing with it the grim consequences of evacuation and isolation from the west.

When the people returned after the liberation they energetically and succesfully rebuilt the city.

Uit de abdij Prüm uit 893, bestaande uit een kerk en een paar bezittingen, is de hoofdstad van de provincie Gelderland ontstaan. Bij de "Slag om Arnhem" tijdens de laatste wereldoorlog was de Rijnbrug "een brug te ver", met alle nare gevolgen van evacuatie en isolatie van het westen van Nederland.

Na de bevrijding teruggekeerd, bouwde de bevolking energiek en met succes de stad weer op.

Aus der aus dem Jahre 893 stammenden Abtei Prüm, die eine Kirche und ein paar Ländereien besaß, entwickelte sich die Hauptstadt der Provinz Gelderland. Bei der Schlacht von Arnhem im letzten Weltkrieg wurde die Brücke von Arnhem als Orientierungshilfe für die alliierten Luftlandetruppen fatal. Evakuierung und Abtrennung vom Westen der Niederlande waren die Folge.

Nach der Befreiung kehrte die Bevölkerung zurück und baute die Stadt tatkräftig wieder auf, mit Erfolg.

La province de Gueldre doit son chef-lieu à l'abbaye Prüm (893), se composant d'une église et de quelques propriétés. Pendant la bataille d'Arnhem de la dernière guerre mondiale, le Rijnbrug (pont du Rhin) était "un pont trop loin", ce qui provoqua l'évacuation et l'isolation de la région.

Revenue après la libération, la population s'est attelée énergiquement et avec succès à la reconstruction de la ville.

Arnhem, capital de la provincia de Güeldres, tiene su origen en la abadía Prüm del año 893 constituida por una iglesia y algunas haciendas. En la 'Batalla de Arnhem' librada durante la última guerra mundial, el puente sobre el Rin fue 'un puente de más', lo que trajo consigo las desagradables consecuencias de la evacuación de los vecinos y el aislamiento del oeste de Holanda.

La población regresó después de la liberación y se entregó con energía y éxito a la reconstrucción de la ciudad.

893年に創立されたプルム僧院は、教会と荘園から成っていましたが、これがヘルダーランド州の首都アーネムの起源でした。第二次世界大戦におけるアーネムの会戦では、アーネムのラインブルグ橋が、「A Bridge Too Far」でした。不幸な撤退とオランダ西部の隔離が、その結果となりました。

終戦後アーネムの住民は、熱意を持って再興に努め、アーネムは再び活気に満ちた都市となりました。

St. Hubertushoeve, Hunting manor

The legend of St. Hubertus and the symbols which changed his life inspired H. P. Berlage, a well-known architect of this century, to design this magnificent hunting manor built in 1920.

Hubertus, a fervant hunter, turned to priesterhood after an encounter with a deer wearing a shining crucifix which cautioned him by saying 'If thou shalt not turn to all that is Godly, hell awaits thee'.

De legende van St. Hubertus en de symbolen, die zijn leven veranderden, werden voor de bekende bouwmeester van deze eeuw, H.P. Berlage, de motieven voor dit prachtige jachtslot uit 1920.

Hubertus - een hartstochtelijk jager - ging als priester verder door het leven na zijn ontmoeting met een schitterend hert, dat een lichtend kruis droeg en hem vermanend toesprak: "Indien gij niet wendt tot wat des geestes is, zult ge ter helle varen."

Die Legende des Heiligen Hubertus und die Symbole, die sein Leben veränderten, wurden für H. P. Berlage - dem international bekannten modernen Architekten - zum Motiv für dieses herrliche Jagdschloß aus dem Jahre 1920.

Hubertus - ein leidenschaftlicher Jäger - wurde durch die Erscheinung eines Hirsches mit einem Kreuz im Geweih bekehrt. Das Tier hatte ihm gesagt: "Wenn du dich nicht dem zuwendest, was des Geistes ist, fahrest du zur Hölle." Er lebte forthin als Priester.

La légende de Saint-Hubert et les symboles qui marquaient la transformation de sa vie, furent les thèmes d'inspiration de ce splendide pavillon de chasse (1920) pour l'architecte renommé H. P. Berlage.

Hubert, chasseur passionné, se fit prêtre après un miracle célèbre: un crucifix lui apparut entre les bois d'un cerf merveilleux qu'il poursuivait et qui le sermonnait: "Si vous ne recourez pas à ce qui est de l'Esprit, vous irez en enfer."

La leyenda de San Huberto y los símbolos que cambiaron su vida sirvieron de temas para este magnífico pabellón de caza construido en 1920 por el famoso arquitecto de este siglo H. P. Berlage.

Humberto - apasionado cazador - se hizo sacerdote después de su encuentro con un ciervo que llevaba una cruz luminosa y le advirtió: "Si no os dedicáis a lo espiritual, iréis al infierno."

聖ヒュベータスの伝説と彼の人生を変えたものの象徴は、今世紀一といわれている有名な建築家H.P.ベルラーハによって、1920年に建てられたこの狩館のモチーフとなっています。

ヒュベータスは狩りを情熱的に愛する男でしたが、ある時光り輝く十字架がある美しい鹿を目撃しました。この鹿が「霊魂のことに心を傾けなくては、汝は地獄に落ちるであろう。」と戒めた以後、ヒューベタスは神父として一生をおくりました。

Nijmegen, Overall view

Nijmegen's location on the river Waal and Meuse-Waal canal has afforded it an important role in navigational traffic between Rotterdam and the German Ruhr district.

The Biblical 'Holy Land Foundation' is situated to the south east of the city. Nijmegen, after Maastricht the country's oldest city, is famous for its splendid architecture.

Door de ligging van Nijmegen aan de rivier de Waal en het Maas-Waal kanaal, heeft de stad een belangrijke functie in het waterwegverkeer tussen Rotterdam en het Ruhrgebied.

Ten zuidoosten van de stad bevindt zich het Bijbels openluchtmuseum "Heilige Land Stichting". Nijmegen, na Maastricht de oudste stad van Nederland, is bekend om zijn vele mooie bouwwerken.

Wegen der Lage an der Waal und dem Maas-Waal-Kanal kommt Nijmegen eine wichtige Rolle beim Schiffsverkehr zwischen Rotterdam un dem Ruhrgebiet zu.

Im Südosten der Stadt befindet sich das biblische Freilichtmuseum "Stiftung des Heiligen Landes". Nijmegen - hinter Maastricht die älteste Stadt der Niederlande - ist wegen seiner vielen schönen Bauten berümt.

Situé sur le Waal et le canal Maas-Waal, la ville de Nimègue occupe une place importante dans le trafic fluvial entre Rotterdam et la Rhur.

Au sud-est de la ville, le musée de plein air de La Bible "Heilige Land Stichting" est situé. Nimégue, la ville la plus ancienne des Pays-Bas, après Maestricht, est réputée pour sa richesse architecturale.

La ciudad de Nimega, por estar situada a orillas del río Waal y del Canal Mosa-Waal, tiene una función importante en la navegación entre Rotterdam y la Cuenca del Ruhr.

Al sureste de la ciudad se encuentra el museo bíblico al aire libre "Heilige Land Stichting". Nimega, después de Maastricht la ciudad más antigua de Holanda, es famosa por sus muchos edificios bonitos.

ワール川とマース・ワール運河に面しているという地理的条件が、ナイメーヘンに、ロッテルダムとルール地域間の水路交通の重要な中間地点としての役割を与えました。

この市の東南には、野外聖書博物館である「聖地協会」があります。オランダ最古の都市マーストリヒトについで、ナイメーヘンは数多い美しい建築物で有名です。

Loevestein Castle

In 1357, near the village of Poederoijen on a spit of land between the merging point of the Meuse and Waal, Dirk Loef van Horne built Loevestein Castle. It served as a state prison for a long period.

The castle gained fame due to the spectacular escape in 1621 of the well-known statesman and lawyer Hugo de Groot. His wife helped him to flee the castle, hidden in a bookcase.

Bij het dorp Poederoijen, op een landtong tussen de samenvloeiing van Maas en Waal, werd in 1357 door Dirk Loef van Horne, slot Loevestein gebouwd. Lange tijd is het een staatsgevangenis geweest.

Bekendheid kreeg het slot door de spectaculaire ontsnapping in 1621 van de bekende staatsman en jurist Hugo de Groot. Met behulp van zijn vrouw wist hij in een boekenkist te ontkomen.

Beim Dorf Poederoijen, auf der Landzunge zwischen dem Zusammenfluß von Maas und Waal, ließ Dirk Loef van Horne im Jahre 1357 Schloß Loevestein erbauen. Das Schloß war lange Zeit ein Staatsgefängnis.

Es wurden durch die spektakuläre Flucht des bekannten holländischen Staatsmanns und Juristen Hugo de Groot im Jahre 1621 bekannt. Dieser entkam mit Hilfe seiner Frau in einer Bücherkiste.

Près du village de Poederoijen, situé sur une langue de terre au confluent de la Meuse et du Waal, Dirk Loef van Horne a bâti le château de Loevestein en 1357, qui a été longtemps prison d'état.

L'homme d'état et juriste Hugo de Groot rendit le château célèbre par son évasion spectaculaire en 1621. Avec l'aide de sa femme, il réussit à s'évader du château dans un coffre à livres.

El castillo de Loevestein fue construido en 1357 por Dirk Loef van Horne. Está situado en una lengua de tierra en la confluencia del Mosa y el Waal, cerca de la localidad de Poederoijen. Durante mucho tiempo ha servido de prisión estatal.

El castillo se hizo famoso por la espectacular evasión, en 1621, del famoso hombre de estado y jurista Hugo el Grande, que con ayuda de su esposa logró escapar en un arca de libros.

1357年に、マース川とヴァール川が交じわる三角州にあるプデロイエン村の付近に、デルク・ルフ・ファン・ホルンは、ルーベスタイン城を建てました。長い期間この城は、国営刑務所として使われていました。

この刑務所の名が一躍広がったのは、1621年に有名な政治家であり、法律家であったヒューゴ・デ・フロートがここから脱出してからです。妻の力を借りて、彼は本用の箱の中に隠れて逃げたのです。

De Efteling, Fairyland

In 1933 two chaplains founded a small, sports complex on the site which today is known as the Efteling, one of Europe's largest and most popular amusement parks.

Except the famous fairytale forest there are many more delights, such as the 'Piraña', a daring stream of rapids, waterfalls and steep rocks.

Van een, door de kapelaans Rietra en de Klijn in 1933 opgericht klein sportcomplex, is de Efteling uitgegroeid tot één van de drukst bezochte en grootste familieparken van Europa.

Behalve het bekende sprookjesbos, biedt de Efteling nog vele andere attracties, zoals de "Piraña", een wildwaterbaan met watervallen, stroomversnellingen en steile rotsen.

Die von den Kaplänen Rietra und De Klijn 1933 gegründete kleine Sportanlage "De Efteling" wuchs allmählich zu einem der meist besuchten Vergnügungsparks Europas aus.

Außer dem bekannten Märchenwald bietet "De Efteling" noch eine Vielzahl anderer Attraktionen an, etwa "Piraña", eine Wildwasserbahn mit Wasserfällen, Katarakten und steilen Felsen.

Issu d'un petit complexe sportif créé en 1933, par les chapelains Rietra et de Klijn, l'Efteling s'est développé jusqu'à devenir un des plus grands parcs d'attractions et de loisirs d'Europe.

Il offre non seulement la forêt aux fées biens connue, mais également un grand nombre d'attractions, telles que le "Piranha", la piste des eaux vives aves ses chutes d'eau, ses rapides et ses rochers raides.

"De Efteling", que era un pequeño polideportivo, fundado en 1933 por los capellanes Rietra y De Klijn, ha llegado a ser uno de los parques de atracciones mayores y más frecuentados de Europa.

Además del famoso 'bosque de cuentos', "De Efteling" ofrece un montón de atracciones; como la Piraña: una pista de agua turbulenta con cascadas, rápidos y afiladas rocas.

1933年にリエトラ及びクライン牧師補によって、スポーツ・センターとして設立されたエフテリングは、ヨーロッパで最も来園者の多い家族遊園地の一つと成長しました。

皆の知っている童話の森以外にも、エフテリングには、岩や滝や急流のあるプール「ピラナ」のような、盛り沢山のアトラクションがあります。

126

Eindhoven, Lightbulbs and soccer

Eindhoven received its municipal rights in 1232 but it remained a small town until the second half of the 19th century with the arrival of the textile and tobacco industry.

It grew significantly however when Philips began manufacturing light bulbs in 1891 which made Eindhoven internationally renowned, not only as 'the city of light', but also because of its succesful soccer team P.S.V.

In 1232 verkreeg Eindhoven stadsrechten, maar het bleef een kleine stad tot in de tweede helft van de 19e eeuw, toen de textiel- en tabaksindustrie hierin verandering bracht.

De echte groei kwam er echter pas in, nadat Philips in 1891 begon met de fabricage van gloeilampen, waardoor Eindhoven uiteindelijk synoniem werd voor lichtstad, doch tevens voor internationaal voetbal (P.S.V.).

Im Jahre 1232 erhielt Eindhoven Stadtrechte. Die Stadt blieb indes bis zur zweiten Hälfte des 19. Jahrhunderts eine kleine Ortschaft. Dann ließ sich hier die Textil- und Tabaksinudstrie nieder, und alles änderte sich.

Das Wachstum beschleunigte sich aber erst wirklich, als Philips 1891 mit der Fertigung von Glühbirnen begann. Seither wird Eindhoven die "Lichtstadt" genannt. Die Stadt wurde aber auch durch die internationalen Erfolge seiner Fußballmannschaft P.S.V. sehr bekannt.

Eindhoven obtint en 1232 ses privilèges communaux, mais aviat conservé son caractère de petite ville jusgu'à la dernière moitié du XIXe s. Les industries du textile et du tabac ont introduit un changement profond.

Eindhoven connut son véritable essor lorsque Philips commença la fabrication des ampoules en 1891, auxquelles elle doit son surnom de "ville de lumière". Et tout le monde sait qu'elle symbolise le football international (P.S.V.).

Eindhoven obtuvo derechos municipales en 1232, pero siguió siendo una ciudad pequeña hasta que, en la segunda mitad del siglo XIX, las industrias de textil y de tabaco la transformaron.

Sin embargo, su crecimiento no fue verdaderamente significante hasta que, en 1891. Philips empezara a fabricar bombillas, por lo que Eindhoven llegó a ser sinónimo de ciudad luminosa, además de ser la fútbol internacional (P.S.V.).

　アイントホーヴァンは、すでに1232年に市としての自治権を獲得していましたが、繊維産業とタバコ産業がこの地で発達する19世紀の後半まで、小規模な市のままでした。
　けれどほんとうの成長は、1891年にフィリップス社が電球の生産を始めてから実現し、アイントホーヴァンは「光の都市」と同名となりました。またこの市は、国際サッカーの分野でも有名です。

Eindhoven, Evoluon

On the edge of Eindhoven against a backround of offices and factories stands Evoluon. Made famous by its exterior as well as its interior design.

The building, designed by engineer L.C. Kalff, was completed in 1966, the 75th anniversary of N.V. Philips Gloeilampenfabrieken. The diameter of the dish is 77 meters and the building is 30 meters high.

Aan de rand van Eindhoven, tegen een achtergrond van kantoorgebouwen en fabriekscomplexen, staat het Evoluon. Zowel door uiterlijke vormgeving als door het interieur kreeg het grote bekendheid.

Het gebouw, een ontwerp van ir. L.C. Kalff, werd in 1966, de 75ste verjaardag van de N.V. Philips Gloeilampenfabrieken, voltooid. De diameter van de schotel is 77 meter en het gebouw is 30 meter hoog.

Am Stadtrand von Eindhoven, vor einem aus Büro- und Fabriksgebäuden bestehenden Hintergrund steht das Evoluon. Sowohl wegen seiner auffallenden Formgestaltung als auch wegen seiner Einrichtung wurde es sehr bekannt.

Das Gebäude, dessen Entwurf von Diplomingenieur L.C. Kalff stammte, wurde 1966 zum 75. Geburtstag der Philips Glühbirnen AG vollendet. Der Durchmesser der Grundfläche beträgt 77 Meter und das Gebäude ist 30 Meter hoch.

Dans la banlieue d'Eindhoven, se détachant sur un arrière-fond d'immeubles de bureaux et de complexes d'unsines, se trouve l'Evoluon, célèbre tant pour son aspect extérieur que pour ses aménagements intérieurs.

Le bâtiment de l'ingénieur L.C. Kalff fut achevé en 1966, pour le 75ième anniversaire des fabriques d'ampoules Philips. La construction parabolique a un diamètre de 77 mètres et une hauteur de 30 mètres.

El "Evoluón" se levanta a las afueras de Eindhoven, con edificios de oficinas y complejos industriales al fondo. Por su especial arquitectura, tanto exterior como interior, obtuvo gran fama.

El Evoluón, diseñado por el ingeniero L.C. Kalff, fue terminado en 1966, el 75⁰ aniversario de la sociedad Philips. El plato tiene un diámetro de 77 metros y la altura del edificio es de 30 metros.

アイントホーヴァン市のはずれの、オフィスビルと工場の群れをバックとしてそびえているのが、エヴォリュオンです。外観そして内部のデザインによって、エヴォリュオンは広く知れわたるようになりました。

この建物は、1966年にL.C.カルフの設計によって、フィリップス株式会社75周年記念として完成しました。円形部分の直径は77メートルで、高さは30メートルです。

130

Willemstad, Fortress

This aerial view shows clearly the magnificent heptagonal star of the Willemstad fortress. Its favourable location on the 'Hollands Diep' encourages tourism in the form of watersports.

The city has a multitude of beautiful old buildings such as the Maurits House built as a hunting lodge for Prince Maurits. It now serves as the town hall. The Willemstad fortress dates from 1583.

De zevenpuntige ster van de vesting Willemstad is schitterend te overzien vanuit de lucht. Bijzonder gunstig gelegen aan het Hollands Diep is er een toenemend watertoerisme.

De stad biedt een schat aan mooie gebouwen, zoals het Mauritshuis, dat werd gebouwd als jachtslot voor Prins Maurits en thans fungeert als stadhuis. De vesting van Willemstad dateert uit 1583.

Der siebenzackige Stern der Festung Willemstad läßt sich aus der Vogelperspektive herrlich überblicken. Wegen der sehr günstigen Lage der Stadt am "Hollands Diep" profitiert die Stadt vom zunehmenden Wassertourismus.

Sie bietet einen reichen Schatz schöner Gebäude, wie das Mauritshaus, das als Jagdschloß für Prins Maurits erbaut wurde und heute Rathaus ist. Die Festung der Stadt stammt aus dem Jahre 1583.

La photo aérienne montre nettement la forme en étoile heptagonale de la ville fortifiée de Willemstad, située dans une position favorable sur le "Hollands Diep" et qui attire un tourisme nautique sans cesse croissant.

La ville offre un trésor de monuments historiques, tels que la mairie Mauritshuis, l'ancien pavillon de chasse du prince Maurits. La forteresse date de 1583.

Desde el aire puede verse perfectamente la estrella de siete puntas de la fortaleza de Willemstad del año 1583. Por su situación privilegiada a orillas del "Hollands Diep", Willemstad goza de un creciente turismo de deportes acuáticos.

La ciudad ofrece abundantes y bellos edificios antiguos, como la Casa de Mauricio, que fue construida como pabellón de caza para el Príncipe Mauricio y que hoy en día sirve de Ayuntamiento.

七角の星型のヴィレムスタッド要塞都市は、上空からの眺めが息をのむようです。ホーランド・ディープに面しているため、水上レジャーと観光に非常に便利です。

この市には、古くチャーミングな建物が多く、ちなみに市庁舎はマオイッツ公が狩館として利用したマオイッツハウスです。ヴィレムスタッド要塞都市は1583年に設立されました。

136

Oudenbosch, The 'small St. Peter'

This Basilica was based on the design of St. Peter's in Rome. The front was modelled on St. John of Lateran, the Cathedral on the Monte Celio in Rome.

The Basilica in Oudenbosch was built by Dr. P. Cuypers and was consecrated on September 14th 1880. On the square is a monument to Pope Pious IX with a zouave.

Deze Basiliek is een ontwerp naar het voorbeeld van de St. Pieter in Rome. Voor de voorkant heeft de St. Jan van Lateranen model gestaan, de Bisschopskerk op de Monte Celio te Rome.

De Basiliek in Oudenbosch is gebouwd door Dr. P. Cuypers en werd op 14 september 1880 ingewijd. Op het plein ervoor staat het monument, voorstellende Paus Pius IX, met een zouaaf.

Der Entwurf für diese Basilika gründet sich auf die Peterskirche in Rom. Für die Vorderseite stand die Lateranbasilika San Giovanni, die Kathedrale des Bischofs von Rom auf dem Monte Celio, Modell.

Die Basilika in Oudenbosch wurde von Dr. P. Cuypers erbaut und am 14. September 1880 eingeweiht. Auf dem Domplatz steht das Denkmal von Papst Pius IX. mit einem Schweizer.

La basilique à été bâtie sur le plan de Saint-Pierre-de-Rome, tandis que le modèle de la façade a été celle de la basilique du Latran, l'église épiscopale sur le Monte Celio de Rome.

La consécration de la basilique d'Oudenbosch construite par le Dr. P. Cuypers, a eu lieu le 14 septembre 1880. Sur la place le monument représentant le pape Pie IX et un de ses zouaves.

Esta basílica ha sido diseñada a imitación de San Pedro de Roma. Para la fachada ha servido de modelo la iglesia episcopal del Monte Celio romano, San Juan de Letrán.

La basílica de Oudenbosch, construida por Dr. P. Cuypers, fue inaugurada el 14 de septiembre de 1880. En la plaza frontal se halla el monumento que representa al Papa Pío IX junto con un zuavo.

この会堂は、ローマのセント・ピーターをモデルとして設計されたものです。聖ヤン・ファン・ラテラーネンの前面は、ローマのモンテ・チェリオの司教教会をモデルとしました。

このアウデンボスの会堂は、P.カウパー博士によって建設され、1880年9月14日に落成しました。会堂の前の広場には、スイス護衛兵を従えたピウス九世法王の像があります。

Maastricht, Capital of the province of Limburg

Around the beginning of the Christian era when the Romans were conquering the Low Lands they founded a settlement on the banks of the Meuse which they called Trajectum ad Mosam.

Later Maastricht and capital of the province of Limburg, it became in the 17th century one of Europe's greatest strongholds. The photograph shows the cheerful Vrijthof with its many pavement cafés.

Omstreeks het begin van onze jaartelling, toen de Romeinen bezig waren de Lage Landen te veroveren, stichtten zij aan de oever van de Maas een nederzetting, die zij Trajectum ad Mosam noemden.

Het latere Maastricht en hoofdstad van de provincie Limburg, was in de 17e eeuw uitgebouwd tot één van de sterkste vestingen in Europa. De foto toont het gezellige Vrijthof, met zijn vele terrassen.

Als die Römer um die Zeitwende Holland eroberten, gründeten sie am Ufer der Maas eine Siedlung, der sie den Namen Trajectum ad Mosam gaben.

Das spätere Maastricht, Hauptstadt der Provinz Limburg, wurden im 17. Jahrhundert zu einer der stärksten Festungen Europas ausgebaut. Das Bild zeigt den gemütlichen Vrythof mit seinen vielen Terrassen.

Au début de notre ère, alors que les Romains conquèraient les Pays-Bas, ils fondèrent, sur la Meuse, une colonie qu'ils appelèrent Trajectum ad Mosam.

Au XVIIe s., elle était devenue une des villes fortifiées les plus importantes de l'Europe et actuellement Maestricht est le chef-lieu de la province du Limbourg. Sur la photo le Vrijthof, place animée à nombreuses terrasses.

A principios de la era cristiana, cuando los romanos estaban conquistando los Países Bajos, fundaron una colonia a orillas del Mosa ya la denominaron Trajectum ad Mosam, la posterior ciudad de Maastricht.

Maastricht, capital de la provincia de Limburgo, se había extendido hasta llegar a ser, en el siglo XVII, una de las fortalezas más fuertes de Europa. La foto muestra la animada Vrythof con sus numerosas terrazas.

ローマ人が今日のオランダにあたる場所を占領しようとしていた紀元の始まりの頃、マース川沿いに居留地を作り、トラジェクタム・アド・モサムと呼びました。

これがその後リンバーグ州の州都マーストリヒトとなり、17世紀にはヨーロッパで最も堅固な要塞の一つとなりました。この写真には、テラス・カフェなどが数多くあって、楽しいふんいきのフライホフが写っています。

Maastricht, Provincial Government Building

The new 'Limburgse Gouvernement', seat of the Limburg provincial government, was built between March 1983 and October 1985. Queen Beatrix conducted the official opening on April 22nd 1986. This new 'Provincial Hall' stands along the river Meuse to the south of the J.F. Kennedy Bridge in the Randwyck district of Maastricht.

Het nieuwe Limburgse Gouvernement, bestuurszetel van het Limburgse Provinciebestuur, werd gebouwd in de periode maart 1983 tot oktober 1985. H.M. Koningin Beatrix verrichtte de officiële opening op 22 april 1986. Dit nieuwe "Provinciehuis" is gebouwd aan de Maas ten zuiden van de J.F. Kennedybrug. De buurt waar het nieuwe Gouvernement in Maastricht staat heet "Randwyck".

Das neue "Limburger Gouvernement", Sitz der Limburger Provinzverwaltung, wurde im Zeitraum März 1983 bis Oktober 1985 erbaut. Königin Beatrix eröffnete das neue Verwaltungsgebäude an der Maas südlich der J.F.-Kennedy-Brücke am 22. April 1986.
Das Gebiet, in dem das neue Gebäude der Provinzverwaltung in Maastricht steht, heißt "Randwyck".

Le nouveau Gouvernement du Limbourg, siège du gouvernement provincial bâti entre mars 1983 et octobre 1985, fut ouvert officiellement par la reine Béatrice le 22 avril 1986. Ce nouveau siège des états provinciaux est situé dans le quartier "Randwyck" de Maestricht, sur la Meuse au sud du pont J.F. Kennedy.

El nuevo edificio del Gobierno de Limburgo, sede de la adminstración provincial, fue construido en el período de marzo de 1983 a octubre de 1985. S.M. la Reina Beatriz realizó la inauguración oficial el 22 de abril de 1986. Esta nueva 'Casa Provincial' está situada a orillas del Mosa, al sur del puente llamado de J.F. Kennedy.
El lugar donde se encuentra el nuevo Gobierno de Maastricht se llama "Randwijck".

　1983年3月から1985年10月にかけて、リンバーグ州の新州庁舎が建設されましたが、1986年4月22日にベアトリックス女王陛下が正式にこの州庁舎をオープンしました。この建物はマース川に面し、J.F.ケネディー通りの南にあたります。
　新州庁舎は、マーストリヒトのランドワイク地域にあります。

Thorn, The 'white village'

Thorn is often called 'the white village' due to its many white-washed houses. A walk through this picturesque village, particularly on a sunny day, is a delightful experience, the cosy streets giving a clear and clean impression.

The 14th century former abbey St. Michael's Church was restored between 1860 and 1885 by P.J.H. Cuypers.

Thorn wordt over het algemeen "het witte dorp" genoemd, daar bijna alle muren van de huizen wit geschilderd zijn. Lopend door de gezellige straten van dit pittoreske dorp, vooral op een zonnige dag, geeft het geheel een heldere en schone indruk.

De 14e eeuwse voormalige abdijkerk St. Michael werd tussen 1860 en 1885 door P.J.H. Cuypers gerestaureerd.

Man nennt Thorn gemeinhin das "weiße Dorf". Denn fast alle Häuserwände sind weiß angestrichen. Bei einem Spaziergang durch die gemutlichen Straßen dieser malerischen Ortschaft, vor allem an einem sonnigen Tage, macht das Dorf auf den Betrachter einen klaren und sauberen Eindruck.

Die aus dem 14. Jahrhundert stammende ehemalige Abteikirche St. Michael wurde von 1860 bis 1885 von P.J.H. Cuypers restauriert.

Une promenade dans le village pittoresque de Thorn, généralement appelé "le village blanc", toutes ses maisons étant peintes de blanc, est une attraction spéciale. Par une belle journée ensoleillée, remarquez sa clarté et sa beauté.

L'ancienne église abbatiale Saint-Michel, datant du XIVe s., fut restaurée par P.J.H. Cuypers entre 1860 et 1885.

Thorn generalmente es llamado "el pueblo blanco" ya que casi todas las paredes de sus casas están pintadas de blanco. Las animadas calles de este pintoresco pueblo dan una impresión de claridad y belleza, sobre todo en un día de sol.

La que fue abadía de San Miguel, del siglo XIV, fue restaurada por P.J.H. Cuypers de 1860 a 1885.

トーンはよく「白い村」と呼ばれますが、それはこの村の家の壁がほとんど全部白にぬられてあるからです。特に天気の良い日に、この絵のような村の愛らしい道を歩いてまわると、すべてが美しく清潔な印象を与えます。

14世紀に設立された元僧院教会であった聖ミカエル教会は、1860年から1885年にかけて、P.J.H. カイパースによって修復されました。

Geleen, DSM

This view of Geleen is dominated by the enormous DSM complex. On this estate of about 800 hectares fertilisers and synthetic materials are produced, as well as raw materials for the pharmaceutical industry and for yarns and fibres. The old village with its early 16th century tower of the Roman Catholic Church of Mercellinus and Peter now lies on the edge of the city. Ancient settlement remains have been found nearby from around 2500 BC.

Deze overzichtsfoto van Geleen wordt overheerst door het enorme bedrijfscomplex van DSM. Op dit terrein van ca. 800 hectare worden o.m. meststoffen, kunststoffen en grondstoffen voor pharmaceutische produkten, alsmede voor garens en vezels vervaardigd. De oude dorpskern, met de vroeg 16e eeuwse toren van de R.K. Kerk Marcellinus en Petrus, ligt thans aan de rand van de stad. Bij Geleen zijn bewoningsresten gevonden van ca. 2500 v. Chr.

Geleen. Panorama einer Stadt und ihrer Industrie. Eine der größten niederländischen Firmen hat sich hier niedergelassen, die DSM. Auf diesem Industriegebiet werden Kunstdünger, Kunststoffe und Grundstoffe für die Pharmaindustrie sowie für Garne und Fasern hergestellt. Der alte Stadtkern verlagerte sich im Zuge der industriellen Neugestaltung an den heutigen Stadtrand. Man erkennt ihn sogleich an dem Turm der katholischen Kirche Marcellinus und Petrus, die aus dem frühen 16. Jahrhundert stammt. In der Nähe von Geleen wurden Überreste der hiesigen Urbevölkerung aus dem Jahre 2500 vor der Zeitwende gefunden.

Le panorama de Geleen montre l'énorme complexe industriel de DSM. Sur un terrain de quelque 800 hectares on produit engrais, matières synthétiques, matières premières pour les produits pharmaceutiques asi que pour les fils à tisser et fibres synthétiques. Le vieux centre du village - remarquez la tour de l'église Saints-Marcellin et Pierre datant du début du XVIe s. - se trouve, de nos jours, aux limites de la ville. Des restes d'habitations datant de ca. 2500 av. J.-C. ont éte trouvés près Geleen.

Esta vista general de Geleen es dominada por el enorme complejo industrial de la empresa DSM. En este terreno de unas 800 hectáreas se fabrican, entre otras cosas, abonos, materiales sintéticos, materias primas para productos farmacéuticos y para hilos y fibras. El antiguo centro del pueblo, con la torre de la iglesia católica Marcelino y Pedro del siglo XVI, se encuentra hoy en día en las afueras de la ciudad. Cerca de Geleen se han encontrado restos de viviendas del año 2500 a.C., aproximadamente.

　ヘレーンの上空写真を独占しているのは、800ヘクタールの敷地をもつ巨大な DSM 会社です。DSM では、肥料、人工繊維、医薬品原料、新素材などを製造しています。
　昔の村の中心は、現在の町のはずれにあたり、16世紀に建てられたカソリック教会マセリナスとペトラスの塔があります。ヘレーンでは、紀元前2500年頃からの村落の遺跡が発見されています。

146

Roermond, Town centre, Meuse view

Roermond was first mentioned in 1130 as a settlement at the mouth of the Roer in the river Meuse. Part of the Hanseatic League, the town flourished economically in the 14th and 15th century through the cloth trade. Nowadays, its industry is centred in and around the Willem Alexander harbour on the Meuse. Roermond's two large yacht harbours indicate its popularity among watersport lovers.

Roermond wordt voor het eerst genoemd in 1130, als nederzetting aan de monding van de Roer in de Maas. Als lid van de "Hanze" kwam de stad in de 14e en 15e eeuw door de lakenhandel in een periode van economische bloei. Nu is de industrie voornamelijk gevestigd in en rond de Willem Alexanderhaven aan de Maas. De twee grote jachthavens geven aan dat Roermond ook geliefd is bij de watersporters.

Roermond wird zum ersten Mal im Jahre 1130 als Siedlung am Zusammenfluß von Roer und Maas erwähnt. Roermond gehörte im 14. und 15. Jahrhundert zu den Hansestädten und erlebte vor allem durch seinen Tuchhandel eine wirtschaftliche Blütezeit. In der heutigen Zeit ist die Industrie hauptsächlich im und am Willem-Alexander-Hafen an der Maas angesiedelt. Allerdings hat Roermond auch zwei große Jachthäfen aufzuweisen, die ein beliebtes Ziel für Wassersportfreunde geworden sind.

La ville de Roermond, ancien membre de la Ligue hanséatique, est mentionnée pour la première fois en 1130 comme colonie au confluent de la Rhur et de la Meuse et connut un essor économique aus XIVᵉ et XVᵉ s. grâce au commerce des draps. Les zones industrielles sont principalement situées au Willem Alexanderhaven sur la Meuse. L'existence de deux grands ports de plaisance témoignent de l'attraction que Roermond exerce sur ceux qui pratiquent les sports nautiques.

Roermond es mencionada por primera vez en 1130, como una colonia situada en la desembocadura del Ruhr en el Mosa. Aliada a la 'Liga de Hansa' llegó a su apogeo económico en los siglos XIV y XV gracias al comercio de paños. Actualmente, la industria está establecida principalmente en y alrededor del puerto del río Mosa llamado de Guillermo Alejandro. Los dos grandes puertos deportivos indican que Roermond es también un lugar apreciado por los aficionados al deporte acuático.

ルアモンドの名の由来は、1130年に遡ることができます。この市は、マース川の河口 (モンド) にある居留地として始まったからです。このハンザ連盟の加盟市の経済は、14世紀から15世紀にかけて、リネン貿易によって栄えました。現在この市の産業は、主にマース川にあるヴィレム・アレキサンダー港を中心としています。またルアモンドには二番目に大きいヨット港があるということが、この市が水上スポーツ・ファンのお気に入りであるということを示しています。

Vaals,
'Where three countries meet'

The Vaals Mountain (322 meters) is the highest point in the Netherlands. Border stones mark the spot where three countries meet: the Netherlands, Belgium and West Germany.
 There is a magnificent view from the Wilhelmina tower.

De Vaalser Berg is met 322 meter het hoogste punt van Nederland. Hier ligt het Drielandenpunt met de grensstenen van Nederland, België en de Duitse Bondsrepubliek.
 Vanaf de Wilhelminatoren heeft men en prachtig uitzicht.

Der Vaalser Berg ist mit seinen 322 m die höchste Erhebung der Niederlande. Hier befindet sich das sogenannte Dreiländereck, auf dem sich die Grenzsteine der Länder Belgien, Bundesrepublik Deutschland und Niederlande vereinigen.
 Vom Wilhelmina-Turm aus hat man eine wunderschöne Aussicht.

Le Vaalserberg, point culminant (322 m) des Pays-Bas, est le point d'intersection marqué par les bornes de trois pays: les Pays-Bas, la Belgique et l'Allemagne de l'ouest.
 De la Tour de Wilhelmine on a une vue splendide.

El Monte de Vaals de 322 metros de altura es el punto más alto de Holanda. Allí se encuentra el 'Punto de los Tres Países', con los mojones fronterizos de Holanda, Bélgica y la República Federal Alemana.
 Desde la torre llamada de Guillermina se disfruta de una vista espléndida.

 ヴァルサー山は322メートルの高さをもって、オランダ一の高さを誇っています。ここには三国境地点があり、オランダ、ベルギー、そしてドイツの国境が交わっています。
 ヴィレミナ・タワーからの眺めは、すばらしいものです。

(Overleaf) Margraten, 'Resting in the alien soil they fought for'

This battlefield cemetery, the only American military cemetery in the Netherlands, was established here on November 10th, 1944 by the U.S. Ninth Army. Here rest 8.301 of the U.S. military Dead, representing 43 percent of those, who were originally buried in this and other temporary cemeteries in this region. Most of them gave their lives to liberate eastern Holland during World War II.

Deze begraafplaats, de enige Amerikaanse begraafplaats in Nederland, werd op 10 november 1944 door het Negende Amerikaanse leger in gebruik genomen. Momenteel liggen hier 8.301 Amerikaanse militairen begraven, dit is 43 procent van het totaal, dat voordien op deze plaats en op andere, tijdelijke kerkhoven bergraven lag. De meeste van hen gaven hun leven bij de bevrijding van Oost-Nederland tijdens de tweede wereldoorlog.

Bei diesem Friedhof handelt es sich um den einzigen amerikanischen Friedhof der Niederlande. Er wurde am 10. November 1944 von der Neunten Amerikanischen Armee in Gebrauch genommen. Momentan liegen hier 8301 amerikanische Soldaten begraben, das heißt 43 Prozent aller Gräber dieser Stätte und von Übergangsfriedhöfen. Die meisten dieser Soldaten starben während der Befreiung des östlichen Teils der Niederlande im Zweiten Weltkrieg.

Au cimetière américain, le seul en Hollande, utilisé pour la première fois par la neuvième armée américaine le 10 novembre 1944, sont enterrés 8.301 militaires américains, 43% de tous les soldats qui ont été enterrés ici et provisoirement dans d'autres cimetières. La plupart d'entre eux ont donné leur vie pendant la deuxième guerre mondiale lors de la libération de la partie orientale du pays.

Este es el único cementerio norteamericano situado en Holanda. Fue usado por el Noveno Ejército norteamericano, a partir del 10 de noviembre de 1944. Actualmente están enterrados aquí 8.301 militares norteamericanos, un 43 por cien del total que estaba antes enterrado en cementerios temporales, como éste. La mayoría de ellos perdieron la vida durante la segunda Guerra Mundial, en la liberación de la parte este de Holanda.

　この戦争墓地は、オランダにおける唯一のアメリカ軍墓地で、1944年11月10日にアメリカ合衆国第九陸軍隊によってできました。ここには8301名のアメリカ軍の軍人死者が葬られていますが、この数は以前この墓地と他の墓地に一時的に葬られたアメリカ人の43%に相当します。この人々のほとんどが、第二次世界大戦中、東オランダの開放のために命を捧げました。

Middelburg, Capital of the province of Zeeland

Middelburg was founded around the 12th century and received municipal rights in 1217. Its strategic position on the island of Walcheren between the waterways of Bruges and Antwerp favourably influenced trade which attracted large numbers of emigrants from Antwerp.

Middelburg boasts 1100 protected buildings putting it in third place after Amsterdam and Maastricht.

Middelburg, ontstaan omstreeks de 12e eeuw, verwierf reeds in 1217 stadsrechten. De strategische ligging op het eiland Walcheren, tussen de vaarwegen van Brugge en Antwerpen, beïnvloedde de handel in gunstige zin. Hierdoor werden veel emigranten uit Antwerpen aangetrokken.

Wat oude monumenten betreft, komt Middelburg met het aantal van 1100 op de derde plaats, na Amsterdam en Maastricht.

Middelburg, um das 12. Jahrhundert entstanden, erhielt bereits im Jahre 1217 Stadtrechte. Ihre strategisch gesehen interessante Lage zwischen Brügge und Antwerpen beeinflußte den Handel und Wandel dieser Stadt in jeder Beziehung. Viele Emigranten aus Antwerpen strömten denn auch herbei.

Mit seinen 1100 historischen Bau- und Kunstwerken steht Middelburg an dritter Stelle, hinter Amsterdam und Maastricht.

Middelbourg, fondée vers le XIIᵉ s., obtint ses privilèges communaux dès 1217. Sa situation stratégique sur l'île de Walcheren, entre les voies navigables de Bruges et d'Anvers, lui assurait une position commerciale favorable. Un grand nombre d'émigrants d'Anvers y furent attirés.

Middelbourg compte 1100 monuments historiques, ce qui lui vaut la troisième place nationale, après Amsterdam et Maestricht.

Middelburg se formó alrededor del siglo XII. Ya en 1217 obtuvo derechos municipales. Su situación estratégica en la isla de Walcheren, entre las vías fluviales de Brujas y Amberes, favoreció mucho el comercio. Esto atrajo a muchos emigrantes de Amberes.

Middelburg ocupa, con sus 1100 monumentos antiguos, un tercer lugar, después de Amsterdam y Maastricht.

　12世紀頃からの歴史をもつミドルバーグは、1217年に市自治権を獲得しました。ブルージュとアントワーペンの間のワルヘレン島にあるこの市は、地の利を得て、貿易の町として栄えました。この町の繁栄に惹かれて、アントワーペンからも多数の移民がやってきました。

　ミドルバーグ内で歴史的建築・遺跡として指定されている数は1100におよび、アムステルダムとマーストリヒトについで第三番目の地位を占めています。

The most ingenious of the Delta Works

The flood barrier in the East Scheldt required know-how and expertise so a thorough study took place concentrating on safety, environment, fishing and shipping.

Gigantic pillars form the backbone of the barrier which was officially opened on October 4th 1986 by Queen Beatrix. The East Scheldt remained open but safety is guaranteed.

De stormvloedkering in de Oosterschelde vereiste kennis en ervaring, die nog moesten worden ontwikkeld. Een uitgebreid onderzoek vond plaats, waarbij veiligheid, millieu, visserij en scheepvaart voorop stonden.

Mammoet pijlers vormen de ruggegraat van de kering, die op 4 oktober 1986 door Koningin Beatrix in gebruik werd gesteld. De Oosterschelde is open gebleven, maar de veiligheid is gewaarborgd.

Das Sturmflutwehr für die Oosterschelde erforderte Know-how und Erfahrung, die man erst noch sammeln mußte. Und so wurde dieser Plan zu einem enormen Forschungsprojekt, bei dem die Sicherheits- und Umweltvorkehrungen mit ebensolcher Gründlichkeit beachtet werden mußten, wie die Belange der Schiffahrt und der Fischerei.

Mammutpfeiler bilden heute das Rückgrat des Sturmflutwehrs, das am 4. Oktober 1986 von Königin Beatrix eingeweiht und seiner neuen Bestimmung übergeben wurde. Die Oosterschelde ist frei zugänglich geblieben, und trotzdem wird hier Sicherheit gewährleistet.

Le barrage anti-tempête dans l'Escaut Oriental demandait des connaissances et de l'expérience qu'il fallait encore acquérir. On entreprit des recherches en donnant la primauté à la sécurité, l'environnement, la pêche et la navigation.

Des piles gigantesques constituent l'essentiel du barrage, mis en service par la reine Béatrice le 4 octobre 1986. L'Escaut Oriental est toujours ouvert, mais la sécurité est garantie.

La presa de contención de mareas vivas que se pretendía construir en el Escalda Este requería unos conocimientos y una experiencia que aún estaban por desarrollarse. Se llevó a cabo una amplia investigación, prestando especial atención a la seguridad, el medio ambiente, la pesca y la navegación.

Enormes pilares forman la espina dorsal de la presa, que fue inaugurada por la Riena Beatriz el 4 de octubre de 1986. El Escalda Este sigue abierto al mar, pero la seguridad está garantizada.

1953年に大洪水があってから、デルタワークと呼ばれるようになった工事が必要とみなされました。東スヘルダー大堤防の建設は、新たに得なくてはならなかった知識と経験を要求しました。安全、環境、漁業、航海などのテーマのもとに、幅広い研究が行われました。

巨大な柱がこの防波堤の背骨となり、1986年10月4日にベアトリックス女王によって、完成式が行われました。この開閉式堤防のおかげで、東スヘルダーの海水を締め切らずに、安全を保証することができるようになりました。

Vlissingen (Flushing)

Due to its location at the mouth of the West Scheldt, the shipping route to Antwerp, Flushing has always been involved in shipping and ship building. The city serves as an auxilliary base for the Royal Dutch Navy and there is also a station belonging to the Belgian and Dutch pilotage service.
Along the boulevard on the Keizersbolevark (Emperor's stronghold) there is a statue of a prominent citizen, the sea hero Michiel Adriaenszoon de Ruyter (1607-1676).

Door de ligging aan de monding van de Westerschelde, de vaarroute naar Antwerpen, is Vlissingen van oudsher bij scheepvaart en scheepsbouw betrokken. De stad doet dienst als hulpbasis van onze Koninklijke Marine en tevens is er een station van de Belgische - en Nederlandse loodsdienst.
Van de in Vlissingen geboren zeeheld Michiel Adriaenszoon de Ruyter (1607-1676) staat een standbeeld aan de boulevard op het Keizersbolwerk.

Vlissingen, die Stadt an der Westerschelde-Mündung, liegt auf der Schiffahrtsroute in Richtung Antwerpen. Es liegt in der Natur der Sache, daß hier eine jahrhundertelange Schiffahrts- und Schiffsbau-tradition das Stadtbild beherrscht. Heutzutage dient die Stadt außerdem als Hilfsbasis der Königlich Niederländischen Marine, und auch der belgisch-niederländische Lotsendienst hat hier seinen Sitz.
Der in Vlissingen geborene Seeheld Michiel Adriaenszoon de Ruyter (1607-1676) wird mit einem Denkmal auf der Promenade beim Keizersbolwerk in Ehren gehalten.

Située à l'embouchure de l'Escaut Occidental, la voie navigable d'Anvers, Flessingue connaît, depuis des siècles, ses activités de navigation et de construction navale. Base auxiliaire de la Marine Nationale, elle sert également de station de pilotage belge et néerlandaise.
Sur le boulevard du Keizersbolwerk, une statue du héros de la mer Michael Adriaenszoon de Ruyter (1607-1676), qui est né à Flessingue.

Vlissingen está situada en la desembocadura del Escalda Oeste, la ruta de navegación a Amberes. Por ello, la ciudad ha estado desde siempre relacionada con la navegación y la construcción naval. Sirve de base auxiliar a la Marina Real holandesa, y cuenta también con una base de prácticos belgas y holandeses.
En el bulevar Keizersbolwerk se encuentra una estatua de Michiel Adriaenszoon de Ruyter (1607-1676), héroe de mar nacido en Vlissingen.

アントワープへの航路がある、西スヘルダー海への口にあたるという地理的条件が、昔から航海と造船をフリシンガンでの要にしてきました。この市には王立海軍の水上援助統括部があり、またベルギーとオランダの水先案内公安があります。
フリシンガン生まれのミヒル・アドリアンスゾーン・デ・ライター（1607-1676）の像が、カイザーボルワークの大通りにあります。

Borssele, Nuclear- and coal power

We take electricity for granted, just a flick of the switch - as long as the light bulb still works. Of course it is not as simple as that. Electricity must be generated at power plants such as this nuclear and coal power station 1 km from Borssele on the south coast of South Beveland in Zeeland.

It is an ideal location due to the port facilities for the supply of coal.

Electriciteit is heel vanzelfsprekend. Met een druk op een knopje is er licht, mits de gloeilamp niet stuk is. Toch komt deze energie niet vanzelf. Het moet worden opgewekt in centrales, zoals in deze kern- kolencentrale op 1 km afstand van Borssele, aan de zuidkust van Zuid-Beveland in Zeeland.

Deze lokatie is van nature zeer geschikt, vanwege de havenfaciliteit voor de aanvoer van kolen.

Eine der selbstverständlich gewordenen modernen Errungenschaften ist die Elektrizität. Ein Anknipsen, ein Drehen, ein Drücken des Lichtschalters und die Nacht wird zum Tag, es sei denn, die Glühbirne versagt ihren Dienst. Die dazu benötigte Energie entsteht jedoch leider nicht von selbst. Sie wird in Kraftwerken erzeugt, wie zum Beispiel in diesem Kern- und Kohlenkraftwerk, das 1 km von Borssele entfernt liegt.

Es hat seinen Standplatz an der Südküste von Zuid-Beveland in Seeland nicht zufällig erhalten, denn hier lassen sich schließlich alle Annehmlichkeiten eines Hafens mit der benötigten Kohlenanfuhr verbinden.

L'électricité est une forme d'énergie évidente: en appuyant sur le bouton, chacun s'attend à la lumière, à moins que la lampe ne soit cassée. Mais sa production est moins évidente. Le courant électrique est produit dans des centrales comme celle-ci, centrale nucléaire et thermique alimentée en houille, située à un kilomètre de Borssele, dans la partie méridionale de Zuid-Beveland en Zélande.

Lieu très approprié à cause des facilités qu'offre le port au transport du charbon.

La electricidad es algo muy normal: apretando un botón se enciende la luz, a no ser que la bombilla esté fundida. No obstante, esa energía no aparece por sí misma. Debe ser generada en centrales, como esta central nuclear y de carbón situada a un kilómetro de Borssele, en la costa sur de Beveland meridional, provincia de Zelanda.

Tiene de por sí una ubicación muy apropiada, por las facilidades del puerto destinado al abastecimiento del carbón.

私達は電気を当たり前のものとしています。電球がきれていない限り、スイッチを押せば光がつく。けれど電気のエネルギーは無からくるものではありません。ゼーランド州の南ベーベランド海岸にあるボーセルから1キロの距離にある、ここの原子力・石炭利用の発電所のような所で電気エネルギーができるのです。

ここには港があって、石炭の輸送に便利なため、発電所の場所として非常に適しています。

Veere, Harbour vieuw

After the Veer gap was closed in 1961 the town's fishing fleet was forced to move elsewhere. Today, the harbour, favourably situated on the Veere lake, is entirely geared to watersports.
The creek district, west of Veere, is a nature reserve and controlled by the state. Veere is a splended town with a host of historic buildings such as the town hall and the Cathedral.

Nadat in 1961 het Veerse Gat werd gesloten, moest de Veerse vissersvloot naar elders uitwijken. Thans is de haven, gunstig gelegen aan het Veerse Meer, geheel ingesteld op de watersport.
Het kreken-gebied, ten westen van Veere, is natuurmonument en valt onder beheer van de staat. Veere is een prachtige Zeeuwse stad, met een keur aan historische gebouwen, zoals het stadhuis en de Dom.

Im Jahre 1961 wurde das sogenannte "Veerse Gat" vom Meer abgeriegelt. Seitdem ist die Fischereiflotte von Veere auf einen anderen Standort angewiesen. Der alte Hafen ist darum heutzutage auf ein ganz anderes Publikum eingestellt, die Wassersportler nämlich, die die günstige Lage an der See von Veere auf ihre Art und Weise zu schätzen wissen.
Das Gebiet westlich von Veere wurde zum Naturschutzgebiet. Veere ist eine wunderschöne Stadt, in seeländischer Tradition erbaut, mit vielen historisch interessanten Gebäuden, zu denen u.a. der Dom und das Rathaus gehören.

Après la fermeture du Veerse Gat, en 1961, la flotille de pêche de Veere dut s'installer ailleurs. Situé favorablement sur le Veerse Meer, le port sert maintenant de port de plaisance.
La région de criques, à l'ouest de Veere, est un site protégé et sous l'administration de l'Etat. Veere est une des belles villes de Zélande, riche en monuments historiques tels que la mairie et la cathédrale.

En 1961 se cerró el que fue brazo de mar Veerse Gat, por lo que la flota pesquera de Veere tuvo que desplazarse a otro sitio. Actualmente, el puerto, con su situación favorable en el Lago de Veere, está habilitado por completo para el deporte acuático.
La zona de calas, situada al oeste de Veere, es monumento natural administrado por el Estado. Veere es una magnífica ciudad zelandesa, con una gran variedad de edificios históricos, como el Ayuntamiento y la Catedral.

1961年にフェール海口が締め切られてから、フェールの漁師は、別の生計を立てる方法を見つけなくてはなりませんでした。それでフェールセ湖にある港を、水上スポーツに利用することになりました。
フェールの西部にある入江地帯は、自然保護地と指定され、国の管理下におかれています。フェールは、ゼーウ地方のきれいな都市でもあり、市庁舎やドムのような歴史的な建物が数多くあります。

The 'Zuid-Beveland' Canal

To provide an efficient and quick shipping route, construction of a canal was started in 1861 between Wemeldinge and Hansweert (foreground).

The canal was completed in 1866 and stretches more than 9 km forming the shortest route to the north for commercial shipping from Gent, Terneuzen and the Sloe area.

Om te kunnen voorzien in een goede en korte verbinding voor het scheepvaartverkeer, begint men in 1861 met de aanleg van een kanaal tussen Wemeldinge en Hansweert (voorgrond foto).

Het kwam gereed in 1866 en is ruim 9 km lang. Voor de handelsscheepvaart van Gent, Terneuzen en het Sloegebied, is dit de kortste waterweg naar het noorden.

Schon im 19. Jahrhundert wußte man in den Niederlanden nichts mehr zu schätzen, als eine gute und schnelle Verbindungslinie für die Schiffahrt. Und so begann man im Jahre 1861 mit dem Bau eines Kanals zwischen Wemeldinge und Hansweert (Vordergrund).

1866 wurden ein beachtlicher, 9 km langer Bau fertiggestellt. Für die Handelsschiffe aus Gent, Terneuzen und aus dem Sloegebiet ist dieses noch immer der kürzeste Wasserweg in Richtung Norden.

Pour répondre au besoin de bonnes et de rapides communications du trafic fluvial, on a entrepris en 1861 la construction d'un canal entre Wemeldinge et Hansweert (premier plan de la photo).

Achevé en 1866 et long de plus de 9 km, il marque la route au nord la plus courte des échanges commerciaux de Gand, Terneuzen et la région de Het Sloe.

Para satisfacer la necesidad de una buena y corta conexión para el tráfico marítimo, se empieza en 1861 con la construcción de un canal entre Wemeldinge y Hansweert (en la foto, en primer plano).

El canal fue terminado en 1866 y tiene una longitud de más de 9 kilómetros. Esta es la vía fluvial más corta hacia el norte, para la navegación comercial de Gante, Terneuzen y el área del Sloe.

ヴェメルディンヘとハンスヴィアートの間の距離を縮め、よい航路とするために、1861年に運河の建設が始まりました。(写真前景)

1866年に完成したこの運河の全長は9キロメートル以上で、ゲント、テヌーゼン、そしてスルー地帯からの貿易船が、この北に向かう短距離航路を利用しています。

The Hague, The Peace Palace

Seat of the permanent Court of Arbitration and the International Court of Justice in The Hague. Founded in 1903 by American Andrew Carnegie it was opened as the Peace Palace in 1913.

Carnegie was born in 1835 in Scotland and emigrated in 1848 with his family to Pittsburgh in Pennsylvania. He became a steel and oil baron. After 1901 he devoted his life to charities, art and education. He died in 1919 as a true philanthropist.

Zetel van het permanente Hof van Arbitrage en van het Internationaal Gerechtshof in Den Haag. Gesticht in 1903 door de Amerikaan Andrew Carnegie werd het als Vredespaleis in 1913 geopend.

Carnegie werd in 1835 in Schotland geboren en emigreerde in 1848 met zijn gezin naar Pittsburgh in Pennsylvania. Hij werkte zich op tot staalmagnaat en oliebaron. Na 1901 zette hij zich helemaal in voor liefdadigheidsinstellingen, kunst en onderwijs. Als een ware filantroop overleed hij in 1919.

Ständiger Sitz des Schiedsamtes und des Internationalen Gerichtshofes in Den Haag. Im Jahre 1903 wurde das Gebäude von dem Amerikaner Andrew Carnegie gestiftet, um dann im Jahre 1913 bei seiner feierlichen Eröffnung den Namen Friedenspalast zu erhalten.

Carnegie wurde 1835 in Schottland geboren und emigrierte 1848 mit seiner Familie nach Pittsburgh, Pennsylvania. Dort machte er als Stahlmagnat und Ölbaron eine typisch amerikanische Karriere. Nach 1901 setzte er sich hauptsächlich für Wohltätigkeitszwecke, für die Kunst und das Bildungswesen ein. Ein wahrhafter Philanthrop, der nach einem erfüllten Leben im Jahre 1919 dahinschied.

Siège de la Cour permanente d'Arbitrage et de la Cour internationale de Justice à la Haye. En 1903, l'Américain Andrew Carnegie offrit les fonds pour le Palais de la Paix, ouvert en 1913.

Né en Ecosse en 1835, Carnegie émigra avec sa famille à Pittsburgh (Pennsylvanie) en 1848. Et il fit fortune: magnat de l'industrie métallurgique et de l'huile, il s'avoue à partir de 1901 aux associations de bienfaisance, aux arts et à l'enseignement. Devenu un véritable philanthrope, il mourut en 1919.

Este Palacio de La Haya fue fundado en 1903 por el norteamericano Andrew Carnegie e inaugurado en 1913 como Palacio de la Paz; es la sede del Tribunal Permanente de Arbitrajes y del Tribunal Internacional.

Carnegie nació en 1835 en Escocia y emigró en 1848 con su familia a Pittsburgh, Pennsylvania. Llegó a ser magnate del acero y del petróleo. A partir de 1901 se dedicó por completo a la filantropía, el arte y la enseñanza. Falleció en 1919, siendo un verdadero filántropo.

これがハーグ市（デン・ハーグ）にある、国際司法裁判所および仲裁裁判所です。この建物は1903年にアメリカ人のアンドリュー・カーネギーによってスタートされ1913年に平和宮（ピースパレス）としてオープンしました。

カーネギーは1835年にスコットランドで生まれ、1848年に家族と共にペンシルバニア州のピッツバーグに移民しました。鋼鉄富豪・石油王となるまで働き続けましたが、1901年以後は、慈善事業と芸術と教育のために献身しました。慈善家カーネギーは、1919年に亡くなりました。

Scheveningen, 'The Pier'

The famous seaside resort of Scheveningen is traditionally a fishing port. Fish is still a major export commodity with herring, cod, haddock, sole, mackerel and plaice crossing the Dutch borders.

The Kurhaus, originally a health centre and bath house for the rich, is now a hotel and casino. The pier is a great tourist attraction, for the Dutch-, as well as people from abroad.

De bekende badplaats Scheveningen is van oudsher vissershaven. Vis is nog altijd een belangrijk exportartikel en behalve haring, gaat er ook kabeljauw, schelvis, tong, makreel en schol de grens over.

Het Kurhaus, oorspronkelijk gebouwd als kuur- en badhuis voor de welgestelden, doet nu nog dienst als hotel en casino. De pier is voor vele Nederlandse- en buitenlandse toeristen, een grote trekpleister.

Scheveningen, einer der bekanntesten Badeorte der Niederlande, war ursprünglich ein kleines Fischerdorf. Auch heute noch ist der Fisch ein wichtiger Exportartikel, und das beschränkt sich nicht nur auf den berühmten Maatjes-Hering. Auch Kabeljau, Schellfisch, Seezunge und Scholle werden von hier aus in viele Länder exportiert.

Das Kurhaus, seinerzeit als Kur- und Badehaus für die oberen Zehntausend erbaut, ist heute ein Hotel mit Casino. Für viele in- und ausländische Touristen ist vor allem der Pier eine besondere Attraktion.

Station balnéaire réputée, Scheveningen était à l'origine un port de pêche. La hareng est toujours un article d'exportation important, mais il n'est pas le seul: cabillaud, églefin, sole, maquereau, carrelet s'y ajoutent.

Le Kurhaus, à l'origine établissement thermal pour les gens aisés, abrite maintenant un hôtel et un casino. Le Pier, longue jetée-promenade attire un grand nombre de touristes néerlandais et étrangers.

La famosa localidad playera de Scheveningen ha sido desde siempre puerto de pesca. El pescado sigue siendo un importante artículo de exportación. Aparte del arenque se exportan bacalao, merluza, lenguado, caballa y platija.

El Kurhaus, en un principio construido como centro de salud y balneario para los ricos, sirve hoy en día de hotel y casino. El malecón de Scheveningen es una gran atracción para muchos turistas holandeses y extranjeros.

有名な海水浴場スヘーベニンゲンは、昔から漁村でした。魚は現在でも重要な輸出品で、にしん以外にも、たら、赤たら、舌びらめ、さば、ひらめ等が国境を越えていきます。

クーアハウスは、もともと金持ちのための治療と海水浴場のホテルとして建てられましたが、現在でもホテルとカジノとして使われています。スヘーベニンゲンのピアーには、オランダ人も外国人もふくめて大勢の観光客が訪れます。

172

'The Glass City', near Monster

Flying across the Westland over the area between the four cities of The Hague, Hook of Holland, Vlaardingen and Delft, we find a gigantic expanse of glass, 'The Glass City'. The aerial view shows just a section, near Monster, of this vast area of hothouses where more than 3000 people are involved in the successful production of flowers, plants, vegetables and fruit in the 'garden of Europe'.

In vogelvlucht over het Westland gaande, gelegen in de stedenvierhoek Den Haag - Hoek van Holland - Vlaardingen - Delft, zien we een reusachtige oppervlakte glas: "De Glazen Stad". De luchtfoto toont een stukje van dit enorme gebied van kassen bij Monster. In totaal werken meer dan 3.000 kwekers met groot succes in de "tuin van Europa" aan de teelt van bloemen, planten, groenten en fruit.

Im Vogelflug über das Westland erblickt man schon von weitem eine enorm große Glasfläche, die "Gläserne Stadt". Sie liegt innerhalb des Städtevierecks Den Haag - Hoek van Holland - Vlaardingen-Delft. Auf dieser Luftaufnahme erkennt man ein Stück aus diesem langgestreckten Gebiet in der Nähe von Monster, auf dem sich Gewächshaus an Gewächshaus reiht. Insgesamt sind hier, im "Garten Europas", mehr als 3000 Gärtner mit dem Blumen-, Pflanzen-, Gemüse- und Obstanbau beschäftigt.

Si l'on survole la région du Westland, située entre les quatre villes de La Haye, Hoek van Holland, Vlaardingen et Delft, on aperçoit "La Ville en Verre", où s'étendent des milliers de serres. La photo montre une petite partie de cette région énorme près de Monster. Plus de 3.000 personnes travaillent dans le "jardin de l'Europe", cultivant fleurs, plantes, légumes et fruits.

Volando sobre la región de Westland, que ocupa el cuadrado formado por las ciudades de La Haya, Hoek van Holland, Vlaardingen y Delft, vemos una gigantesca superficie de vidrio: la así llamada 'Ciudad de Vidrio'. La fotografía aérea muestra, en las cercanías de Monster, un trocito de esa inmensa zona de invernaderos. En el también llamado 'Jardín de Europa', un total de más de 3.000 agricultores cultivan con éxito flores, plantas, verduras y frutas.

鳥の目でウエストランドを見下ろすと、デン・ハーグ、フック・ファン・ホーランド、フラーディガン、そしてデルフトの四都市が四角となっている中に、巨大な面積を占めるガラス、「ガラス都市」が目に入ります。この航空写真には、モンスター付近の大きな温室地帯の一部が写っています。3000人以上の栽培者が、「ヨーロッパの庭」で花、観葉植物、野菜と果物を栽培しています。

174

Leidschendam, Prince Claus Traffic Square

The former two-storey flyover on the National highway 12 was improved between 1978 and 1985. Now known as Prince Claus Traffic Square its four-storeys provide an optimal distribution of traffic. The Dfl. 220 million junction is used by 210,000 vehicles each day.
This spectacular construction was opened in 1985 by Queen Beatrix.

De vroegere rotonde in Rijksweg 12, bestaande uit twee verdiepingen, werd van 1978-1985 voor een betere doorstroming en verdeling van verkeer, uitgebreid tot het huidige Prins Claus Verkeersplein met vier verdiepingen. Dit ƒ 220 miljoen kostende verkeersplein verwerkt 210.000 auto's per etmaal.
Het spectaculaire bouwwerk werd in 1985 door H.M. Koningin Beatrix geopend.

Früher befand sich an dieser Stelle der Reichsstraße 12 ein zweistöckiger Verteilerkreis. Zwischen 1978 und 1985 baute man eine gänzlich neue Verkehrsader, um so den Verkehr einerseits besser zu verteilen und andererseits besser durchströmen lassen zu können. Dieses enorme Vorhaben ist das vierstöckige Prinz-Claus-Autobahnkreuz. Der Knotenpunkt wurde mit einem Kostenaufwand von 220 Mio. Gulden erbaut und "verarbeitet" nun täglich an 210.000 Fahrzeuge.
Im Jahre 1985 wurde dieses spektakuläre Bauwerk von Königin Beatrix eröffnet.

L'ancien rond-point de la Route Nationale 12 comptait deux étages. Entre 1978 et 1985, on a porté le nombre d'étages à 4 pour permettre un meilleur écoulement et une meilleure répartition de la circulation. Baptisé Rond-point Prins Claus, ayant coûté fl. 220 millions, il reçoit 210.000 voitures par jour.
La construction imposante a été ouverte par Sa Majesté, La Reine Béatrice, en 1985.

En los años de 1978 a 1985, la rotonda de tráfico de la carretera nacional 12, compuesta de dos niveles, fue ampliada a cuatro niveles y se denominó Rotonda de Tráfico del Príncipe Claus; con ello se aseguraba un mejor tránsito y distribución del tráfico; actualmente pasan por ella unos 210.000 vehículos diarios. La rotonda ha costado 220 millones de florines.
La espectacular obra fue inaugurada en 1985 por S.M. la Reina Beatriz.

以前国道12号のロータリーは、二段式になっていましたが、車の循環の改善にため1978年から1985年にかけて、四レベルのプリンス・クラウス交通プラザが建設されました。この2.2億ギルダーかけた道路システムは、24時間に21万の車をさばきます。
このダイナミックな道路建設は、1985年にベアトリックス女王陛下によって開通されました。

The river Lek, 'Like a silver ribbon'

The river Lek winds its way like a silver ribbon through the Dutch countryside, flowing along the southern boundary of the province of Utrecht with the provinces of Gelderland and South Holland.

In the 8th century a river flowed to the west of Wijk bij Duurstede which was called Lockia. In the year 1100 the 'Kromme Rijn' was dammed so that the Lek became the main tributary of the Rhine measuring 61 km in length.

Als een zilver lint slingert de rivier Lek zich door het Nederlandse landschap, stromend op de zuidgrens van de provincie Utrecht, met de provincies Gelderland en Zuid-Holland.

Ten westen van Wijk bij Duurstede stroomde een water, dat in de 8e eeuw als Lockia vermeld wordt. In 1100 werd de Kromme Rijn afgedamd, waarmee de Lek de hoofdstroom van de Rijn werd met 61 km lengte.

Wie ein silbernes Band schlängelt sich der Fluß Lek durch die niederländische Landschaft, und bildet die Südgrenze, die die Provinz Utrecht von den Provinzen Gelderland und Süd-Holland trennt.

Westlich des Städtchens Wijk bij Duurstede strömte einst ein Flüßchen, das im 8. Jahrhundert bereits unter dem Namen Lockia erwähnt wurde. Im Jahre 1100 nun wurde der "Kromme Rijn" abgedämmt, und so wurde die Lek mit einer Länge von 61 km zum Hauptstrom vom Rijn.

Comme un ruban d'argent le Lek serpente à travers le paysage hollandais en coulant à la frontière du sud de la province d'Utrecht et des provinces de Gueldre et Hollande Méridionale.

A l'ouest de Wijk bij Duurstede se trouvait un cours d'eau nommé le Lockia, mentionné au VIIIᵉ s. Grâce à l'endiguement en 1100 du "Kromme Rijn", le Lek, long de 61 km, est devenu l'affluent principal du Rhin.

Como una cinta de plata, el río Lek serpentea por el paisaje holandés, en la frontera sur de la provincia de Utrecht con las provincias de Güeldres y Holanda del Sur.

Al oeste de la localidad de Wijk bij Duurstede había un arroyo que en el siglo VIII se conocía por el nombre de Lockia. El río "Kromme Rijn" fue cerrado con diques en 1100, por lo que el Lek, con una longitud de 61 kilómetros, se convirtió en la corriente principal del Rin.

銀色のリボンのようにレック川は、ヘルダーランドと南ホーランド州からユトレヒト州の南境に流れ入り、オランダ風景画をくねり通っていきます。

ワイク・ファン・デューアステーデの西に、この八世紀にはロキアと文献に記された川は流れ込みます。1100年にクロマ・ラインがダムでせき止められて以来、全長61キロのレック川は、ライン川の主要支流となりました。

Rotterdam, Skyline

The port of Rotterdam grew tremendously after the war and due to the dedication and insight of those responsible surely deserves its classification as the world's largest port. In the old inland harbour on the north bank (right on photo) virtually all quayside activities have come to a halt. Highrise flats and office blocks now preside.

De haven van Rotterdam is na de oorlog enorm gegroeid en heeft door de inzet en het inzicht van de mensen, die er zo hard aan gewerkt hebben, het volste recht op de positie van wereldhaven nummer één. In de oude binnenhaven zijn op de noord-oever (rechts op de luchtfoto) bijna geen laad- en losactiviteiten meer te bespeuren. Hier bevinden zich thans woontorens en kantoorgebouwen.

Der Hafen von Rotterdam entwickelte sich nach dem Krieg enorm. Mit Einsatz, Tatkraft und Einblick in die Materie verhalfen die Menschen, die dort hart gearbeitet haben, dem Rotterdamer Hafen zu seiner Spitzenposition als Welthafen Nummer Eins. In dem alten Binnenhafen am Nordufer (rechts auf der Luftaufnahme) finden nahezu keine Lade- und Löschaktivitäten mehr statt. Hier sind heutzutage Wohntürme und Bürogebäude angesiedelt.

Après la guerre, le port de Rotterdam a connu un développement énorme. Grâce à l'ardeur et l'intelligence de tous ceux qui s'y sont adonnés, Rotterdam peut se vanter d'être le premier port du monde. Sur le quai du nord (à droite sur la photo) dans le vieil arrière-port, on n'aperçoit plus guère d'activités de chargement ou de déchargement. Ici se trouvent maintenant les grandes tours et les immeubles de bureaux.

El puerto de Rotterdam ha crecido enormemente después de la guerra y tiene pleno derecho a su condición de puerto número uno del mundo, gracias a la dedicación y a las claras ideas de la gente que tanto ha trabajado en ello. En la ribera norte del viejo puerto interior (a la derecha de la fotografía aérea) ya casi no se observan actividades de carga y descarga. Ahora se encuentran allí torres de viviendas y edificios de oficinas.

戦後ロッテルダム港は、市民の絶大な努力とビジョンのおかげで、世界一の港という地位を獲得する程成長しました。北岸に以前の内港であった場所には、もう積み荷ののり下ろしのような活動は、ほとんど目にすることはできません。ここは高層住宅とオフィス街になり、大きな白い建物ネッドロイド本社が、ヴィレム橋の上から突き出ています。

Rotterdam, ECT-docks

This aerial photograph shows the Alexander Terminal for containers of Europe Combined Terminals. ECT is facing the challenge of the eighties and nineties through constant innovation.

Efficiency directed innovations, such as: double action cranes, multi-trailer transport systems, infrared data-communication and computer aided shipplanning.

Deze luchtfoto toont de Alexander Terminal voor containers van Europe Combined Terminals. ECT gaat de uitdaging met de tachtiger en negentiger jaren aan door constante vernieuwing.

Vernieuwing door efficiëntere werkmethoden, zoals: dubbele actie kranen, multi-trailer transport systemen, infrarode data-communicatie en computer gestuurde verschepingsvoorbereiding.

Auf dieser Luftaufnahme erkennt man den Alexander-Container-Terminal, der zu den "Europe Combined Terminals (ECT)" gehört. Die ECT, eine Art Transeuropäische Umschlagsorganisation, weiß sich den Herausforderungen der 80er und 90er Jahre mit seinen ständigen Erneuerungen zu stellen.

Dabei geht es um Erneuerungen auf dem Gebiet effizienterer Arbeitsmethoden, wie z.B. doppelte Arbeitskräne, Multitrailer-Transportsysteme, infrarote Datenübertragung und computergesteuerte Verschiffungsvorbereitung.

La photo montre le Terminal Alexander pour les conteneurs d'Europe Combined Terminals. ECT relève le défi des années 80 et 90 en se renouvelant constamment.

Il se renouvelle en utilisant des méthodes de travail efficaces, telles que: grues à double action, systèmes de transport aux multi-semi-remorques, téléinformatique par infrarouge, préparation commandée par ordinateur du transport par bateau.

Esta fotografía aérea muestra la Terminal Alexander, para contenedores de Europe Combined Terminals. La empresa ECT acepta el reto de los años ochenta y noventa renovándose constantemente.

Esta innovación tiene lugar por medio de métodos de trabajo más eficientes, como grúas de doble acción, sistemas de transporte en remolques múltiples, comunicación de datos por rayos infrarrojos y preparación del embarque dirigida por ordenador.

この航空写真に写っているのは、ヨーロッパ・コンバインド・ターミナル(ECT)のアレキサンダー・ターミナルです。ECT は、1980年代と90年代のチャレンジに応えるべく、絶え間ない革新に努めています。

ダブル・アクション・クレーン、モルチ・トレイラー運搬システム、赤外線データ通信、コンピュータ化された運輸プラン作成などによる、常に現状にマッチした能率化を ECT は目指しています。

182

Rotterdam, Europoort oil-docks

The aerial view shows part of the oil storage and refineries, so common in Rotterdam, on the 4th Petroleum dock with Shell Nederland's refinery in the background.

Also in the field of petrochemicals, Rotterdam has every right to call itself the gateway of Europe, but in general the Europoort project is a result of structural changes in world trade.

De luchtfoto toont een deel van de olie-opslag en raffinaderijen, die Rotterdam rijk is, aan de 4e Petroleumhaven, met een raffinaderij van Shell Nederland op de achtergrond.

Ook op het gebied van de petrochemie, mag Rotterdam zich met recht de poort van Europa noemen, doch algemeen is het Europoort-project een gevolg van de structurele veranderingen in de wereldhandel.

Öllagertanks und Raffinerien, eine typische Rotterdamer Hafenszene. Hier hat man einen Blick auf den vierten Petroleumhafen mit einer Raffinerie von Shell Nederland im Hintergrund.

Auch auf dem Gebiet der Petrochemie darf Rotterdam sich zu Recht das Tor Europas nennen. Letzten Endes ist das Europoort-Projekt jedoch eine Folge struktureller Veränderungen des Weltmarktes allgemein.

Sur la photo, on aperçoit une partie des réservoirs à pétrole et des raffineries situés dans le quatrième Port Pétrolier de Rotterdam. Une raffinerie de Shell Nederland se voit sur l'arrière-plan.

Même dans le domaine de la pétrochimie, Rotterdam occupe une place importante. Et s'il pourrait se nommer, à juste titre, la Porte de l'Europe, le projet Europoort est pourtant considéré être le résultat de changements structurels dans le commerce mondial.

La fotografía aérea muestra una parte de los almacenes y refinerías de petróleo que abundan en Rotterdam, en el 4⁰ Puerto del Petróleo, con una refinería de Shell Nederland al fondo.

En el campo de la petroquímica, Rotterdam también puede ser calificada como la puerta de Europa con todo derecho, pero en términos generales, el proyecto de Europoort es una consecuencia de los cambios estructurales del comercio mundial.

　この上空写真は、シェルの精油所をバックに、第四石油港にある、ロッテルダムに数多くある石油貯蔵タンクと精油設備の一部を表しています。

　石油化学品分野においても、ロッテルダムはヨーロッパの玄関口といえましょう。ロッテルダムのユロポート計画は、世界の新しい動向をキャッチしています。

184

Rotterdam, Europoort ore-docks

A colourful part of the world's largest port, the ore container dock of Europoort C.V. processes 24 million tonnes of iron ore each year. Together with the EMO on the Meuse plain, a total of 39.5 million tonnes of iron ore is shipped to Rotterdam each year from all over the world.

The ore is shipped further, primarily via inland waterways, to countries such as Germany, France, Austria and Belgium.

Als een kleurig onderdeel van 's werelds grootste havengebied, verwerkt de erts overslaghaven van Europoort C.V. 24 miljoen ton ijzererts per jaar. Samen met de EMO op de Maasvlakte, betekent dit een totaal-aanvoer van ijzererts in Rotterdam van 39,5 miljoen ton per jaar, vanuit alle werelddelen.

Hoofdzakelijk per binnenvaart, wordt het erts doorgevoerd naar o.a. Duitsland, Frankrijk, Oostenrijk en België.

Die Erzverladung, ein besonders farbenfrohes Stückchen des größten Hafengebietes der Welt. Hier beim Europoort C.V. werden zirka 24 Mio. Tonnen Eisenerz pro Jahre verladen. Damit erhält Rotterdam, zusammen mit EMO im Mündungsgebiet der Maas, eine Eisenerz-Gesamtanfuhr von 39,5 Mio. Tonnen pro Jahr aus allen Teilen der Erde.

Die Erze werden hauptsächlich von Binnenschiffen weiter transportiert, wie z.B. nach Deutschland, Frankreich, Österreich und Belgien.

Partie multicolore de l'ensemble portuaire le plus grand du monde, le port de transbordement de minerais (Europoort C.V.) reçoit 24 millions de tonnes de minerai de fer par an. Les arrivages de minerai à Rotterdam, venant de toutes les parties du monde, comptent, y compris ceux d'EMO dans la Plaine de la Meuse, au total 39,5 millions de tonnes par an.

Les minerais sont ensuite transportés, par navigation fluviale, dans des pays tels que l'Allemagne, la France, l'Autriche et la Belgique.

Como una parte de colores vivos de la zona portuaria mayor del mundo, el puerto de transbordo de minerales de la sociedad Europoort C.V. elabora 24 millones de toneladas de mineral de hierro al año. Esto supone, junto con el EMO en la llanura del río Mosa, un abastecimiento total de mineral de hierro de 39,5 millones de toneladas al año, desde todas las partes del mundo a Rotterdam.

El mineral es conducido luego a Alemania, Francia, Austria y Bélgica, entre otros países, principalmente por navegación fluvial.

世界一大きな港地帯のカラフルな一部として、ユロポート C.V. 積換港は、年間2400万トンにおよぶ鉄鉱石を処理しています。マースフラクテにある EMO と合計すると、ロッテルダムにおける世界各国からの鉄鉱石輸入量は、年間3950万トンとなります。

主に内陸水路によって、鉱石はドイツ、フランス、オーストリアなどに運ばれてゆきます。

Hook of Holland, 'Where ferries come and go'

The construction of the 'Nieuwe Waterweg', a canal completed in 1872, provided Rotterdam with a direct link to the North Sea. This resulted in two coastal villages, Oude Hoek and the stately Nieuwe Hoek. The Zeeland Ferry company has maintained a service to Harwich for more than a century. September 1st, 1989 it was taken over by the Stena Line, which operates two vessels, the Queen Beatrix (see photo) and the St. Nicholas.

Door de aanleg van de Nieuwe Waterweg, een in 1872 voltooid kanaal, ontstond voor Rotterdam een rechtstreekse verbinding met de Noordzee. Zo ontstonden er aan de kust twee dorpen, Oude Hoek en het villapark Nieuwe Hoek. Vanuit Hoek van Holland heeft de Mij. Zeeland meer dan honderd jaar een ferry-verbinding met Harwich onderhouden. Per 1 spetember 1989 is dit overgenomen door de Stena Line, die met twee schepen, de Koningin Beatrix (zie luchtfoto) en de St. Nicholas, opereert.

Der Bau des "Nieuwe Waterweg", der im Jahre 1872 fertiggestellt wurde, war ein wichtiger Schritt auf dem Wege zu Rotterdams günstiger Hafenlage, denn damit wurde eine direkte öffnung zur Nordsee geschaffen. Gleichzeitig entstanden an der Küste zwei Dörfer, und zwar Oude Hoek und der Dorfpark Nieuwe Hoek. Die Schiffahrtsgesellschaft Zeeland hat mehr als hundert Jahre lang die Fährverbindung zwischen Hoek van Holland und Harwich geregelt. Seit dem 1. September 1989 wurde der Fährdienst jedoch von der Stena Line mit den beiden Fähren Königin Beatrix (siehe Luftaufnahme) und St. Nicolas übernommen.

La construction du canal le Nieuwe Waterweg, achevée en 1872, a créé pour Rotterdam une liaison directe avec la mer du Nord. Ainsi sont nés deux villages, Oude Hoek et le parc résidentiel Nieuwe Hoek. Pendant plus de cent ans, la cie Zeeland a entretenu une ligne de ferry-boat entre Hoek van Holland et Harwich. Le 1er septembre 1989, ce service a été pris en charge par la Stena Line opérant avec deux bateaux, La Reine Béatrice (voir la photo) et le Saint-Nicolas.

Con la construcción del Nieuwe Waterweg, un canal que fue terminado en 1872, se formó un enlace directo entre Rotterdam y el Mar del Norte. De esa forma se originaron dos pueblos en la costa, Oude Hoek y el parque residencial Nieuwe Hoek. La compañia Zeeland ha mantenido durante más de cien años un enlace de ferry de Hoek van Holland a Harwich. A partir del 1 de septiembre de 1989 se ha hecho cargo de ello la Stena Line, que opera con dos barcos: el Reina Beatriz (véase la fotografía aérea) y el San Nicolás.

　1872年に完成した「新水路」運河によって、ロッテルダムは北海と直接つながれるようになりました。そして岸には、アウワ・フックと一軒建の家が並ぶニューワ・フックの二村ができました。ゼーランド会社は100年以上にわたって、フック・ファン・ホーランドと英国のハリッチをフェリーでむすんでいましたが、1989年9月1日からステナ・ラインが「ベアトリックス女王号」(写真) と「聖ニコラス号」の二船をもって、この業務を受け継ぎました。

Hellevoetsluis Harbour

In November 1688, Prince William III left Hellevoetsluis with an armada of 370 ships for Torbay in England. King James of England fled and William and Mary Stuart became King and Queen of England and Scotland. This historical development resulted in the Netherlands remaining an independent nation as these three countries formed a united strength against French King Louis XIV.

Vanuit Hellevoetsluis vertrok in november 1688 Stadhouder Prins Willem III, aan het hoofd van een armada van 370 schepen, waarmee hij een geslaagde landing uitvoerde bij Torbay in Engeland. De Engelse koning Jacobus vluchtte voor zoveel machtsvertoon en zo werden Willem en Mary Stuart koningspaar van Engeland en Schotland. Dankzij deze daad zijn de Nederlanden onafhankelijk gebleven, aangezien deze drie naties een verenigde kracht vormden tegen de Franse koning Lodewijk XIV.

Der Stadthalter Prinz Wilhelm III., ist November 1688 als Führer einer 370 Schiffe starken Armada von Hellevoetsluis aus in Richtung England aufgebrochen und eroberte dort die Stadt Torbay. Angesichts einer solchen Machtdemonstration flüchtete der englische König Jakob, was zur Folge hatte, das Wilhelm und Maria Stuart das Monarchenpaar von England und Schottland wurden. Mit dieser Tat stellten die Niederlande weiterhin ihre Unabhängigkeit sicher, denn zusammen mit England und Schottland waren die Niederlande für Frankreichs Ludwig XIV. zu einer uneinnehmbaren Festung geworden.

En novembre 1688, le stathouder prince Guillaume III partit de Hellevoetsluis, à la tête d'une armada de 370 navires, avec laquelle il débarqua avec succès à Torbay en Angleterre. Le roi d'Angleterre Jacques dut céder devant une telle manifestation de force et ainsi Guillaume et Mary Stuart occupèrent les trônes de Grande-Bretagne et d'Ecosse. Grâce à ces événements, les Pays-Bas ont pu rester indépendants, ces trois nations constituant une puissance unie face au roi de France Louis XIV.

En noviembre de 1688 partió de Hellevoetsluis el Magistrado Supremo Príncipe Guillermo III, al frente de una armada de 370 buques, con los que efectuó con éxito el desembarque en Torbay, en Inglaterra. Ante tanta ostentación de poder, el rey inglés Jacobo huyó y así Guillermo y María Estuardo se transformaron en la pareja real de Inglaterra y Escocia. Gracias a este hecho, los Países Bajos continuaron siendo una nación independiente, ya que estas tres naciones formaban una fuerza unida contra el rey francés Luis XIV.

1688年11月総督ヴィレム三世は、370隻の艦隊を率いてヘルスフットスラウスから出発し、イギリスのトーベイに上陸するのに成功しました。
イギリスのジェームス王は、ヴィレム三世の艦隊の勇姿に驚いて逃亡したので、ヴィレムとメリー・スチュワートは夫婦として、イギリスとスコットランドの統治者となりました。この結果オランダは国としての独立を守ることができ、イギリス、スコットランド、オランダの三国が力を合わせることによって、フランス王ルイ十四世との対抗が可能となったのです。

190

Barrage near Hagestein, One of the early Delta Works

Behind the new sea wall in the south of the Delta region is a vast fresh water basin. The level and quality of the water is regulated, among other things, by this barrage built in 1958 in the Rhine. Other barrages involved are those at Amerongen (1966), Driel (1970) and large outlet locks at the Haringvliet dam.

Achter de nieuwe zeeweringen in het zuidelijk Deltagebied, bevindt zich een uitgestrekt zoetwaterbekken. De stand en kwaliteit van het water in dit bekken wordt o.a. gereguleerd door deze stuw in de Rijn uit 1958. Verder door de stuwen bij Amerongen (1966), Driel (1970) en de enorme uitwateringssluizen in de Haringvlietdam.

Hinter der modernen Küstenbefestigung im südlichen Deltagebiet befindet sich ein weit ausgestrecktes Süßwasserbecken. Der Wasserstand und die Qualität dieses Beckens werden u.a. durch diese Stauanlage im Rijn aus 1958 geregelt. Aber auch die Stauanlagen bei Amerongen (1966), Driel (1970) und die enorm großen Entwässerungsschleusen aus dem Haringvlietdam tragen zu dieser Regulierung bei.

Derrière les nouvelles digues de mer dans la partie méridionale de la plaine deltaïque, se trouve un vaste bassin d'eau douce. Ce barrage dans le Rhin de 1958 est un des barrages qui régularisent le niveau et la qualité des eaux du bassin. Quelques d'autres barrages: celui d'Amerongen (1966), de Driel (1970) et les grandes écluses d'évacuation du Barrage du Haringvliet.

Detrás de los nuevos diques, en la zona sur del Delta, se encuentra una extensa cuenca de agua dulce. El nivel y la calidad del agua de la cuenca son regulados por esta presa del Rin de 1958 y además por las presas de Amerongen (1966), Driel (1970) y las enormes esclusas de desagüe de la presa de Haringvliet.

　デルタ地帯南部の新しい海洋堤防の後に、大規模な淡水ため池があります。このため池の淡水の状態と質は、1958年に設置されたライン川のダムによって調節されています。このダム以外にも、アメローガン（1966年）とドリール（1970年）のダムと、ハーリングフリートダムの巨大な排水用水門によって水質調整が行われてれいます。

Utrecht, Capital of the province of Utrecht

It is not surprising that Utrecht's central location in the Netherlands has resulted in its being the centre of Dutch Railways. It is also the major trade fair city. The aerial view shows clearly the Hoog Catharijne, a magnificent heart of shops and offices with, in the background, the Dom - the Netherlands' highest tower at 112 metres.

Vanwege de centrale ligging in Nederland, is het niet verwonderlijk dat Utrecht - behalve Jaarbeursstad -, tevens het centrum is van de Nederlandse Spoorwegen. De luchtfoto geeft een mooi overzicht van Hoog Catherijne, het winkel- en kantoorhart van Nederland. Daarachter verheft zich de alom bekende Dom, met de hoogste toren van Nederland (112 m .).

Die Stadt Utrecht ist aufgrund ihrer zentralen Lage in den Niederlanden nicht nur als wichtige Messestadt von Belang. Sie ist auch Hauptverkehrsknotenpunkt der niederländischen Eisenbahn. Diese Luftaufnahme bietet einen gelungenen Überblick über Hoog Catharijne, dem großen Einkaufs- und Geschäftszentrum der Niederlande. Dahinter ist der Turm des berühmten Utrechter Doms zu erkennen, der gleichzeitig der höchste Turm der Niederlande ist (112 m).

Située en plein centre des Pays-Bas, la ville d'Utrecht, réputée pour son palais des Expositions, est également le centre des Chemins de Fer néerlandais. Sur la photo un beau panorama sur le nouveau centre commercial Hoog Catharijne. Situé au coeur du pays, il renferme des galeries commerçantes et des immeubles de bureaux. Derrière s'élève le Domtoren, campanile très connu et le plus haut du pays (112 m).

A causa de su ubicación en el centro de Holanda, no es extraño que Utrecht sea el centro de los Ferrocarriles Holandeses, además de ser también la ciudad de las Ferias de Muestras. La fotografía aérea ofrece una bonita vista general de Hoog Catherijne, el corazón comercial y de oficinas de Holanda. Detrás se eleva la catedral, conocida por todos, con la torre más alta de Holanda (112 m.).

オランダの真ん中にあるという地理的条件を考えると、ユトレヒトにオランダ鉄道統括本部があり、ヤーバース大見本市会場があるということも頷けます。この上空写真では、オランダでも主要なショッピングセンターおよびオフィスビルセンターである、ホーフ・カタライナの美しい全景が見られます。その裏にはオランダ一高い塔、有名なドム（高さ112メートル）がそびえています。

Nieuwegein, Shopping centre

Nieuwegein, à young municipality in the province of Utrecht, came into being on July 1st 1971 as a result of the merging of the two municipalities of Vreeswijk and Jutphaas.

The aerial view of the shopping centre illustrates its progressive character with experimental architecture.

Nieuwegein, een nog zeer jonge gemeente in de provincie Utrecht, werd gevormd op 1 juli 1971 en is onstaan door de samenvoeging van de gemeenten Vreeswijk en Jutphaas.

Als een moderne, vooruitstrevende gemeente, durft men met excentrieke bouwstijlen te experimenteren, zoals te zien is op deze luchtfoto van het winkelcentrum.

Nieuwegein, eine noch sehr junge Gemeinde in der Provinz Utrecht. Sie wurde am 1. Juli 1971 gegründet und setzt sich aus den ehemaligen Gemeinden Vreeswijk und Jutphaas zusammen.

Es ist eine moderne und vorwärtstrebende Gemeinde, die gern mit exzentrischen Baustilen experimentiert, wie beispielsweise auf dieser Luftaufnahme vom Einkaufszentrum zu erkennen ist.

Nieuwegein, commune encore très jeune de la province d'Utrecht, reçut son nom le 1er juillet 1971 et naquit de la fusion des communes de Vreeswijk et Jutphaas. Modernes et progressistes, ses habitants osent essayer différents styles d'architecture. En témoigne cette photo du centre commercial.

Nieuwegein, un municipio muy joven en la provincia de Utrecht, se formó el 1 de julio de 1971 y surgió por la unión de los municipios Vreeswijk y Jutphaas.

Como corresponde a un municipio moderno y progresista, se experimenta con excéntricos estilos de arquitectura, tal como se puede apreciar en esta fotografía aérea de las galerías comerciales.

ニューウェハインは、ユトレヒト州でも非常に若い町で、1971年7月1日にフレースワイクとユットファースを合併して創立されました。近代的な前向きの町として、この上空写真のショッピングセンターに見られるように、ニューウェハインではエキセントリックな建築スタイルを実験する勇気も持ち合わせています。

The Loosdrecht Lakes

The Loosdrecht lake district is a peat area in the province of Utrecht covering some 2125 hectares. A truly magnificent part of the country frequented by watersport lovers and campers.

It looks as if all the sailing boats find their own course without the help of traffic signs- or lights.

De Loosdrechtse Plassen is een veenplassengebied in de provincie Utrecht van ca. 2125 hectare. Een enorm mooi gebied, waar het voor kampeerders en watersport liefhebbers heerlijk toeven is.

Zo te zien lijkt het alsof al die zeilboten, varende zonder een vast patroon, verkeerstekens of -lichten, toch hun eigen weg weten te vinden.

Die Loosdrechtse Seenplatte liegt in einer Moorlandschaft der Provinz Utrecht. Dieses zirka 2125 Hektar große und wunderschön gelegene Gebiet ist ein beliebtes Ausflugsziel für Wassersportler aller Art.

Wie man sieht, finden all die Segelboote, die sich kreuz und guer über das Wasser fortbewegen, auch ohne Verkehrszeichen und Ampeln ihren Weg.

Les lacs de Loosdrecht occupent d'anciennes tourbières de ca. 2125 hectares dans la province d'Utrecht. Une région extrêmement belle, particulièrement propice aux sports nautiques et aux campeurs.

Il semblerait à première vue que ces voiliers, naviguant chacun à sa guise, sans aucune signalisation, trouvent pourtant leur chemin.

Loosdrechtse Plassen es una región de lagos de turberas de alrededor de 2125 hactáreas, en la provincia de Utrecht. Es una región extremadamente bella, donde campistas y amantes del deporte acuático disfrutan de una excelente estancia.

A juzgar por las apariencias, parece como si todos esos veleros que navegan sin un patrono fijo, sin señales de tráfico o semáforos, sepan encontrar aun así su propio camino.

ユトレヒト州ロードレフトは、泥炭採掘によってできた湖地帯です。約2125ヘクタールにおよぶ、とても美しいこの場所には、キャンパーや水上スポーツ・ファンが訪れて楽しい時を過ごしています。

こうして見ると、ここに写っているヨットは、交通標識も信号もなしに迷うのではないかと心配ですが、それぞれ方向をつかんで舵をとっているようです。

'All's well that ends well'

The Houtribdyke, Lelystad-Enkhuizen, at sunset. This charming picture is surely an appropriate ending to a photo book of the Netherlands. I hope you had a pleasant and interesting flight.

H. Siliakus

De Houtribdijk, Lelystad-Enkhuizen, bij zonsondergang. Het leek mij passend, een fotoboek van Nederland met deze fraaie typerende opname te besluiten. Hopelijk heeft U een prettige en interessante vlucht gehad.

Der Houtrib-Deich, Lelystad-Enkhuizen, im Sonnenuntergang. Eine prächtige, typisch holländische Szene, die, wie mir scheint, ein würdiger Abschluß dieses Bildbandes ist. Ich hoffe, Sie hatten einem angenehmen und interessanten Flug.

La digue Houtrib, Lelystad-Enkhuizen, au coucher du soleil. Il m'a paru convenable de terminer un livre de photographies des Pays-Bas par cette belle vue. J'espère que votre vol a été agréable et intéressant.

El dique de Houtrib, Lelystad-Enkhuizen, a la puesta del sol. Me pareció apropiado el terminar un libro de fotografías aéreas de Holanda con esta hermosa fotografía típica. Espero que haya tenido usted un vuelo agradable e interesante.

エンクハウゼンとレリースタッドの間にあるハウトリブデックの日没。この写真で、オランダ写真集を閉じるのが最適ではないでしょうか。皆様が、このフライトをお楽しみになったことを祈っています。